"Here is a book we need: a real look into what it means to be a caregiver. By sharing her family's journey, Jenny Lisk has given us both a poignant memoir as well as a de facto guide for the otherwise uncharted waters of caring for a loved one through illness and the healthcare system. Taking us stepwise from the time of her husband's diagnosis through his wrenching and inevitable death, all while raising two kids, Jenny gives us an invaluable peek into both the practicalities and the emotional mettle such a travail can summon in a person."

—**BJ Miller, MD, Hospice & Palliative Medicine Physician, Author, and Founder of Mettle Health**

"Nobody wants to be a future widow or widower. But when that inevitability looms, you want a trusted guide to hold your hand. Jenny Lisk's debut memoir is just that. You get her reports from the front lines which teach you the nitty gritty of caring for your partner, your kids, and maybe even yourself as things get tougher. You get her reflection years hence on what was really going on in those moments, and important lessons learned. Thanks to Lisk, you learn that what you are going through is normal, that you will survive it, and that you are not alone. Frank, tender, real, and ultimately optimistic, *Future Widow* is the ultimate gift for someone going through the unthinkable."

—**Julie Lythcott-Haims, *New York Times* bestselling author of *How to Raise an Adult* and *Real American***

"From the moment Jenny Lisk's husband was diagnosed with terminal brain cancer, she knew her life would undergo a tectonic shift. In *Future Widow*, she reveals how she navigated the often conflicting priorities of Wife and Mother and she reflects on what she might have done differently, especially if she'd known the distinctive ways children grieve and ultimately heal. Lisk's honesty is both compelling and instructive."

—**Allison Gilbert, author of *Passed and Present* and *Parentless Parents***

"In her gripping personal account of caring for her terminally ill husband, Jenny Lisk illustrates through her lived experience how to maintain hope and, at the same time, prepare for an unwanted future. *Future Widow* is a testament to existing in the present while anticipating the future, being graceful with ourselves when we fall short, and celebrating small victories along the way."

—**Justin Yopp, PhD, Psycho-Oncologist, author of *The Group: Seven Widowed Fathers Reimagine Life***

"A profoundly moving memoir and resource, this book provides a guide for future or current widows and widowers who are parenting grieving children. Jenny Lisk gives an unflinching account of caregiving for her dying husband while raising her young children. I wish my mother had this book in 1974, after losing my dad to cancer when I was a teenager."

—**Mary Robinson, MA, CT, CNN Hero and Founder and Executive Director, Imagine, A Center for Coping with Loss**

"In this heartbreaking and heartwarming book, Jenny Lisk describes the battle of her husband's life against glioblastoma. As a physician involved in her husband's care, I was touched at many levels to be part of the story. Jenny managed to maintain her composure as a mom, wife, and professional throughout this arduous journey. This book provides valuable insights into dealing with personal loss and coming out on the other side, and shares a behind-the-scenes account of caring for a critically ill spouse that will be helpful to healthcare providers and families alike."

—**Charles S. Cobbs, MD, Director, Ivy Center for Advanced Brain Tumor Treatment, Swedish Neurosciences Institute**

"It's been said that one person's survival story becomes another person's survival guide. With *Future Widow* Jenny Lisk has written that and so much more. This isn't just a story of surviving—it's also a story of thriving."

—**Gina Warner, Founder, Badass Women's Book Club**

"Wow. Jenny Lisk writes, with honesty and even a wearying sense of humor, about how to live one life as you know that it is ending, in preparation for this new, unwanted future you would, with all your soul, ask to avoid. Her vivid, human recounting of trying to be a loving partner to her dying husband, even as her heart breaks, is riveting, real and all too relatable, the kind of stuff you tell your friend in a late-night call when no one can hear you cry. Stunning."

—**Leslie Gray Streeter, author of *Black Widow: A Sad/Funny Journey Through Grief for People Who Normally Avoid Books with Words Like 'Journey' in the Title***

"Jenny Lisk poignantly shares the reality her family faced after her husband's glioblastoma diagnosis. She answers questions that often go unasked and offers insights that are painful to comprehend. Her honest accounts of everything from dealing with hijacked intimacy with her spouse to uncertainty about parenting provide brave examples of doing hard things that many will never encounter. For those who do, and those who support them, her reflections provide solace and connection."

—Micki Burns, PhD, Chief Clinical Officer, Judi's House

"In this absorbing memoir Jenny Lisk shares her eight-month journey as she juggled being the full-time caregiver to her husband Dennis, diagnosed with terminal Glioblastoma, while parenting two young children and working full time. Jenny assembled a network of family and friends who buoyed her as she found the strength to face each day. *Future Widow* offers a view of life inside a family impacted by terminal cancer that will inspire and help others heading down that road."

—Lauren Schneider, LCSW, Clinical Director of Child and Adolescent Programs, OUR HOUSE Grief Support Center

"In her amazing book, Jenny Lisk shares her journey as wife and mother, to caregiver of her terminally ill husband, to widowed parent who sought the resources to heal her family after her husband's death. Jenny's honest reflections are real, heartbreaking, and inspiring. Sprinkled throughout are helpful tips for caregivers about things she wished she had known at the time. For those in similar circumstances, Jenny shines a light, showing there is hope and support despite the difficulties."

—Buffy Peters, Director, Hamilton's Academy of Grief & Loss

FUTURE WIDOW

FUTURE WIDOW

LOSING MY HUSBAND, SAVING MY FAMILY, AND
FINDING MY VOICE

JENNY LISK

BLUHEN BOOKS

Future Widow:

Losing My Husband, Saving My Family, and Finding My Voice

ISBN: 978-1-7356136-0-4 (paperback)

978-1-7356136-1-1 (hardcover)

978-1-7356136-2-8 (ePub)

Library of Congress Control Number: 2020922645

Edited by: Jocelyn Carbonara

Cover design by: 100covers.com

Published by: Bluhen Books, Bellevue, Washington

In Loving Memory

Dennis Wilfred Lisk, Jr.
1971-2016

CONTENTS

FOREWORD

JANA DECRISTOFARO, LCSW

This book is one you never want to have to read. It's also the book everyone should read.

Like Jenny, I'm a kid of the 1980s. Throughout my nineteen years of education, grief wasn't on the syllabus for even one class. There was no instruction on what it means to have your world smashed apart by a test result or devastating words from a medical professional. There were no class discussions about how to feel when there's an empty chair at the dining table or how to pick which photos to display at a memorial service. No lessons on how to navigate the healthcare system, ask for help from friends and family, or talk with children about the heartbreak of a dying parent. I learned a lot in school, but not about how to show up for myself and others when grief is at play.

It wasn't until I started volunteering with The Dougy Center for Grieving Children & Families, as a facilitator for a group of teens grieving the death of a parent or sibling, that I realized just how much I didn't know about what it means to have someone die. Or, how to keep living when they do. Over the course of six months, I sat in a small, basement room listening to these teens talk about their people who died. What they missed about them.

What they never got to do with them. What they regretted and wished they'd done or said differently. How they felt alone and misunderstood by friends who "didn't get it." I also listened as they laughed, made connections, shared memories, and supported each other as they traversed significant days like birthdays, graduations, holidays, and the anniversary of their person's death.

What I learned from these teens I couldn't have learned in a classroom. The grief they shared with each other, and with me, didn't fit neatly into the theories, or "stages of grief," models that most traditional education systems teach. As both a volunteer and now an eighteen-year staff member at The Dougy Center, I've listened to thousands of children, teens, young adults, and adults talk about the heartbreak, confusion, numbness, anger, sadness, and every other emotion possible that comes with grieving their person.

The Dougy Center started in 1982 and was the first program in North America to provide grief support groups for children and teens grieving the death of a parent, sibling, primary care-giver, or close friend. Over time, people began asking, and we began asking ourselves, "What about families dealing with a diagnosis? Don't they need support too?"

In 2014, we launched our Pathways Program for families like Jenny's: families facing an advanced serious illness. In the groups for kids, teens, caregivers, and the person with the illness, participants can talk, play, laugh, and cry with other people who, on some level, understand what they're going through. For an hour and half, every other week, when someone asks, "How are you?" these families can give the real answer. If they choose to give that real answer, they can trust they will be met with understanding, and not the unsolicited advice or plati-tudes that are habitual in other environments.

Why do children and teens need this type of support? Well,

what I experienced as a child of the 1980s hasn't changed very much. Most people still don't learn about grief or what's needed when someone is facing a loss—at least not until it happens to them, or someone close to them. That's why places like The Dougy Center, and books like this one, are needed. They give people whose lives are getting smashed apart someplace to go, or something to read, that helps them feel less alone—and maybe a little less lost.

As part of my work at The Dougy Center, I host and produce our podcast, Grief Out Loud. Jenny and I met in 2019 when I reached out about the potential of doing an episode swap. The number of grief podcasts out there is pretty small, so I was surprised that someone else had one focused on a topic most people run away from. When I first saw the title of Jenny's show, "The Widowed Parent Podcast," I thought it was exactly what the families at The Dougy Center needed to hear. After having Jenny on Grief Out Loud, I was struck by her drive to find answers, and create a roadmap both for herself and others who face the confusing landscape of raising grieving children as a suddenly solo parent.

Future Widow is part of that roadmap. It offers a window into not only caregiving for a spouse, but figuring out how to live without them when they die. When you're caregiving for someone with an advanced serious illness, there's rarely time or space to reflect on what is happening; there's just doing what needs to happen next. By looking back on the CaringBridge entries Jenny wrote throughout her husband's illness, she can reflect on the meaning behind those necessary actions and decisions—emotionally, physically, mentally, and spiritually.

That's part of the magic of Jenny's memoir: her willingness to be so transparent. Grief is messy and confusing. It's also transformative and catalyzing. Jenny writes about all those aspects, without falsely shining up the messy parts. This memoir is an honest account of what it's like to sort through the wreckage while holding the contradictions that so often accompany grief: the beauty of community coming together, the ugliness of watching someone we love die, the awe of seeing children and teens find their way, and the pride we feel at how we are transforming.

Through it all, Jenny discovers the strength of her community, her voice, and her capacity for growth—while showing others how to do the same.

Jana DeCristofaro, LCSW
Community Response Program Coordinator
Host of the Grief Out Loud podcast
The Dougy Center for Grieving Children and Families

PREFACE

Today is the first day of August, and the first day of my new challenge: write one thousand words a day for my first book. It's a memoir, based on my CaringBridge journal from the eight months when my husband, Dennis, was battling terminal brain cancer.

When I was planning this endeavor, I thought, *no problem, this will be fun.* I like writing, after all, and I like a good challenge.

Today, however, on Day One, I'm procrastinating. This probably means I'm afraid of something.

What I am afraid of? I don't know. Maybe wrestling with memories from that period. Maybe the sheer amount of time I'll need to put in. Maybe that I won't convey a theme and story that resonates, or helps anyone.

I decided that I will wear my favorite shirt every day for the duration of this challenge. So, if you run into me in August, don't be surprised if I show up in it. Every time. (Fortunately, Amazon is bringing me two more identical shirts tomorrow to reduce the laundry cycling.)

The shirt says, "Nevertheless, She Persisted." I'm not wearing it to make a political statement. I'm wearing it because it reminds me that I'm strong. It reminds me that I can rise to the challenge. It reminds me that I can persist, despite losing my husband to cancer—and losing my imagined future.

It is my hope that you, reader, will persist, too.

Jenny Lisk
August 1, 2019

PART I

OUR LIFE WAS PERFECTLY NORMAL

1

THE DAY LIFE AS I KNEW IT ENDED

When you finally arrive home on a Friday evening—one kid in tow, the other successfully deposited with the Boy Scouts for the weekend and your forty-something-year-old husband has a funny look on his face, your first thought is unlikely to be:

This time next year I'll be a widow, raising two grieving kids alone.

At least, that certainly was not *my* first thought.

After fighting the cross-town traffic characteristic of Seattle's suburbs, I got home one night to find Dennis sitting on the couch in our living room. He had a *look* on his face. I can't really describe it, except to say it was that look that said something was wrong.

The sort of look you recognize after sixteen years of marriage.

I thought something had happened at work, or maybe something else had gone wrong that day. My read of his face was more "pissed off" than "terminally ill."

"What's up?" I asked, my measured tone belying my concern.

"I've been feeling a little dizzy lately."

I sat down on the couch and peppered him with questions.

What are you noticing? When did it start? How often are you feeling dizzy?

He described some slight and occasional dizziness over the previous few days. Nothing dramatic. No I-can't-stand-up moments. No blacking out; nothing that would ring alarm bells.

Since it was after hours, going to see his regular doctor wasn't an option. Nothing about the situation suggested I needed to take him to the emergency room, or even to urgent care. We decided that Dennis should call his doctor on Monday, and we talked about times when I could go in with him.

Somehow, my tagging along seemed like it could be important. Little did I know how true my hunch would prove to be.

Within two weeks, I would become his full-time caregiver.

After we established a plan for next steps, I went to get takeout. Being a Friday after a busy week of normal life—with eight- and ten-year-old kids, and both of us working—we were ready to crash.

When I came back twenty minutes later, I checked in:

"How are you doing? How are you feeling?"

My can-do approach had kicked in, and I wanted to know— had anything changed?

Dennis turned to me and said, "I'm doing OK. But I've been a bit dizzy the past few days."

I stopped. Something about the way he said it sounded like he thought he was imparting new information.

I sized him up. Carefully, I said, "You know, you just told me that."

"I did?"

"Yes. We were right there, on the couch. We had a whole discussion about how you'd been feeling a bit dizzy at times, how you were going to call your doctor on Monday, what days I could come with you. Then I went and got takeout, now I'm back..." I trailed off.

"We did?"

Shit.

Did he really not remember this discussion, just twenty minutes prior?

What is going on?

"Yes."

Calm on the outside. Totally perplexed inside.

I spent the rest of the weekend observing the situation. Mostly, he seemed normal. Now I was second-guessing myself: Was I imagining things? Was I overreading the situation?

What the hell is going on?

Looking back, I think I knew on some level that something was very wrong.

Megan's First Communion was that weekend, and we had a lot to do to prepare. We planned to hold the brunch at my parents' house, even though they were out of town, because our kitchen was torn up with an unexpected remodel brought on by extensive water damage. On Saturday, I told Dennis to stay home and relax, and keep Megan company, while I went to my parents' house to spend the day baking quiche and making the other necessary preparations.

He was supposed to retrieve Peter from Scout camp on Saturday evening, so he'd be there for the Sunday event; but I did that, too. Somehow it didn't seem quite right to send Dennis on the hour-plus-each-direction drive that night.

On Monday morning, Dennis went to work as usual. He called his doctor for an appointment, and he got one—three weeks out. I don't know what he told the scheduler that led to this far-off date being selected. I suspect he described feeling a bit dizzy. He may not have mentioned the confusion.

Perhaps he didn't even remember it.

That evening, he reported back that he'd made an appointment with the doctor. When he told me the date, my gut reaction was that he needed to be seen sooner. But, still, he was *mostly* acting normal. I spent the next week constantly trying to assess: *At what point do I need to intervene? At what point do I call the doctor myself and move up the appointment?*

Thus began eight months of cancer. Eight months of caregiving. Eight months with more questions than answers.

Eight months of hell.

2

FRANKLIN FALLS

The following Sunday, nine days after Dennis first mentioned feeling a bit dizzy, was Mother's Day. We went on a day hike. The first—and last—time I've been to Franklin Falls. It's beautiful, and it's under an hour from my home. I have no desire to go back.

We stopped at the waterfall, which was the midpoint of the outing. The kids splashed with their cousins in the water. Dennis turned to me and said, "Where are we staying tonight?"

Ummm—at home?

"Where do you think we stayed last night?" I carefully asked.

"I don't know. Some cabin in Oregon."

What the hell?

"We were at home last night. This morning we got up, drove to my sister's house, and got in her car. Then we drove thirty minutes up Snoqualmie Pass, and now we're on a hike at Franklin Falls."

"We did?"

I don't know what this is. But this is bad. It's time for me to step in; time for me to call his doctor.

On the return to the car, we had to scramble back up a short

section of a semi-dangerous path—narrow, with a steep drop-off
—to get from the falls to the hiking trail. Dennis held Megan's
hand as they climbed. It haunts me now when I think of what
could have happened, had he slipped or gotten confused on the
way back up.

On Monday, as soon as I could get a break in the chaos of work
—and overseeing the kitchen contractors—I called his doctor's
office. I reached the nurse line and left a message. Tuesday
morning, the nurse called me back. I described Dennis's symptoms and relayed the various odd interactions over the prior
week.

"Bring him in today," the nurse said. "We'll make room for
him."

I was convinced that the symptoms could be attributed to a
medication he'd recently started for a minor issue. I'd been
Googling everything I could think of, including looking up the
side effects of this medication. And there it was, on the list of
uncommon side effects: *cognitive confusion.* Not one of the
common problems, to be sure—but on the list, nonetheless.

I was certain we'd go into his primary care doctor's office,
relay all these odd anecdotes, and come out with a medication
change—and all would once again be well.

The doctor ordered an MRI.

We went downstairs to radiology, and they gave us their
usual instructions: "Wait here, he'll be done in about an hour.
We'll call you in twenty-four hours with the results."

At the end of the hour, they said, "Actually, don't go home
just yet. The doctor would like to see you."

I don't know what this means, but this can't possibly be good.

We went back up to the doctor's office. By this time, it was
after five o'clock.

"There's something really wrong with your brain," he said. "I don't want to scare you, but I think you need to know what you might be dealing with. It might be glioblastoma. You need to see the neurosurgeon tomorrow."

I leaned back and closed my eyes. I was sitting on the visitor's bench in the exam room; Dennis was on the table, and the doctor was on his swivel stool.

"Are we really having this conversation?" I said out loud.

It was truly inconceivable. I walked in thinking Dennis needed a simple medication change, and instead the doctor was sending him to the neurosurgeon. Urgently. I didn't even know what glioblastoma was at that point, but the doctor's demeanor and directions left no doubt—this was bad.

Probably as bad as it gets.

3

THE JOURNEY BEGINS

The next day, we saw the neurosurgeon, Dr. Charles Cobbs, at the Ben and Catherine Ivy Center for Advanced Brain Tumor Treatment. It is part of Swedish Medical Center in Seattle.

Our visit to Dr. Cobbs that day was, for me, the start of many trips across the lake to the Swedish Cherry Hill campus. Office visits. ER visits. Visiting Dennis on the inpatient floors. Sitting in the waiting room, awaiting visits from the surgeon with updates. So, so many visits.

If hearing the internal medicine doctor say, "There's something really wrong with your brain," didn't convey the seriousness of the situation, arriving at the Ivy Center left no doubt. We stepped off the elevator to come face to face with a large sign: "The Ivy Center for Advanced Brain Tumor Treatment."

Does that mean advanced tumors, or advanced treatment?

I couldn't shake the thought.

Less than two weeks ago, my husband was perfectly normal ... and now he has a brain tumor? How can this be our life?

Soon Dennis and I—together with our parents—were in Dr. Cobbs's office. "We need to do surgery right away," he said, after explaining the large mass he saw on the MRI. "We'll do it tomorrow."

His nurse set us up with pre-op instructions. In addition to fasting, there was a special shampoo Dennis needed to use in the morning. It was some sort of anti-bacterial wash, necessary because his skull was to be cut open that day.

That night, we Googled "glioblastoma." What we found was horrifying. It's an extremely aggressive brain cancer. The survival rate is very, very low. Basically, we learned, it was a death sentence.

We were both too overwhelmed to do anything but go to sleep that night. Meaningful conversations, presumably, could be had later. Physical intimacy could wait for another day.

Oh, how wrong those assumptions turned out to be.

Thursday, we awoke to a busy school morning. Normally I was already up and working by 5:00 or 6:00 a.m., since my corporate technology job involved collaborating remotely with an East Coast team. Dennis would get the kids up and ready, and drop them at school on his way to work.

I had abruptly stepped away from my own work earlier in the week—first saying that I needed to take my husband into the doctor, and later following up to convey the gravity of the situation and the uncertainly in front of us.

So, on this particular morning, I was in charge. I had to get four of us ready to go—and get one of us ready for brain surgery. I woke up the kids and got them going. I relayed to Dennis the very specific instructions for using the special shampoo: use it last, and put nothing on your skin after. No lotion, no aftershave, not even deodorant, if I recall correctly.

In the middle of the morning chaos, our home phone rang. My first thought was *I don't have time to talk to anyone right now.*

But then I saw the caller ID: it was my neighbor, whose own husband had died of glioblastoma a few years earlier. I didn't really know her at that point, but a mutual friend told her of our situation, and she was calling to check in. I made time to grab that call.

She asked who our doctor was, and upon hearing the answer, said, "That's exactly where you need to be. You're in the best hands." And, she added: "Remember, this is a marathon, not a sprint. I know that brain surgery feels like a big deal today, and it is. But this is just the beginning. Pace yourself."

I would soon find out how right she was.

Shortly after hanging up the phone, I found Dennis shaving.

Nothing on your skin after using the special shampoo, I shrieked —to myself.

Out loud, I reminded him—calmly—of the nurse's instructions, and persuaded him to stop. Clearly, the brain cancer was already affecting him in insidious ways. This ordinarily competent man couldn't remember the nurse's instructions, even though I'd reviewed them with him fifteen minutes earlier.

They had only given us enough shampoo for one wash, so re-showering wasn't an option. I wasn't sure what would happen, but we had to get the kids to school and get into traffic to make our way to the hospital on time.

When we dropped the kids at school, they did a normal, "Bye! Love you!" type of departure, and hurried off to class. After all, at that point, we only knew that Dennis had a "brain tumor"—scary, to be sure—but we didn't yet know whether it was malignant, or whether it might be fixable. Only much later —after he died—did Megan say how much that interaction continues to haunt her. If she'd known that was the last time she'd really see her dad as himself—that he'd never be the same again—she would have said a proper goodbye.

We got to the hospital and checked Dennis in for the surgery. After they wheeled him away, I joined family—parents and siblings on both sides—in the hospital lobby, which served as the waiting room. There wasn't much to do, but what I remember is this: sitting on my phone and scrolling through the news. Endlessly.

Facebook executive Sheryl Sandberg's husband had just died two weeks earlier. It had been all over the news, and I had followed with the interest of an uninvolved observer: *Poor Sheryl and her kids. How sad for them. I can't imagine.*

All of a sudden, it was personal.

This very well could be me soon. I'd better pay attention.

Even this early in the journey, I had the feeling I needed to follow Sandberg's story closely, to learn from it what I could.

After what seemed like most of the day, the neurosurgeon, Dr. Cobbs, came out to speak with us. Dennis was out of surgery and in the ICU. We could go up later to see him. I don't remember much of what he said; what I do remember was the doctor's kind and compassionate manner, and the time he spent answering questions from every family member present.

Even though very few answers were available at that point.

Up to this point, I had been updating a few close friends by text on the goings-on at the hospital that day. When someone suggested creating a page on the popular online journal, Caring-Bridge, to post updates, I balked initially. I figured I'd keep sending texts and emails to keep people updated.

Pretty quickly, it became obvious this would be unsustainable.

And so, on day one of this ordeal, as we waited for surgery

news, my sister created a page on the site. She did the first post or two, sharing that Dennis was out of surgery and would be in the intensive care unit that first night.

After that, I took over responsibility for posting. It was important to me to share the updates with our community myself.

It ended up being a lifeline for me, to process what was happening in writing, as we lived it.

What follows are my CaringBridge posts from the time Dennis was sick, along with reflections I've added now, five years later.

It is my hope that sharing my family's journey through this health crisis—a time when life turned inward and upside down —will be helpful to your family, too.

PART II

THE JOURNAL, THE JOURNEY

4

Moved to regular floor
May 15, 2015

Dennis moved this afternoon from ICU to a room
on the regular neuro floor. He is eating well
and trying to rest. Father Gary came by to see
us earlier, which was much appreciated. Thanks
to everyone for your help and support.

My first post was so matter-of-fact. So to-the-point.
Dennis is out of ICU.
He's eating.
He's resting.

It felt important to post this update in order to relay the situation on the ground to those who cared about us.

I had no idea at this point that blogging was about to become my vehicle for speaking to my corner of the world. My refuge in a time of crisis and chaos.

My way of making sense of what was happening with us, to us, and for us.

The first night Dennis was in the hospital, he stayed in the intensive care unit. It seemed less-ICU-like than I would have imagined. The room was small. There were various monitors, but I don't remember those as the defining feature of the setup.

I do remember a visitor chair that folded down into a bed. It was small. The mattress was uncomfortable. But it was flat, and I was glad to have it. My poor sister—who stuck around to support me in any way she could—grabbed a fleece blanket from her car, wadded up her jacket as a pillow, and borrowed a spot on the cold, hard floor.

I also remember getting very little sleep that night. Dennis kept waking up and trying to get out of bed. Not remembering that the oxygen monitor needed to stay on his finger, he repeatedly pulled it off. When he removed it, beeping ensued—and I woke up. I felt like I had to leap up and put the monitor back on his finger *immediately*.

Maybe I'd watched too much of the television show *ER* in my younger years, but it seemed like *hospital machines sounding alarms* was a bad thing.

The following day, Dennis was moved from the ICU to an inpatient room. He was on the fifth floor of the hospital, where the neuro patients were cared for.

The fifth floor was about to become a very familiar place.

That first night, however, it was all foreign to me. I hadn't stayed overnight in a hospital since I blew out my knee in a high school basketball game some twenty-five years before—an unfortunate incident which ended my junior year season early and required major reconstructive surgery.

This time—not being the patient myself—I wasn't sure exactly where I fit in. The bathroom in Dennis's room had a sign on it saying, "Patients Only." The first several times I needed to go, I dutifully made the trip down the hall to the visitors' restroom.

Finally, a kind nurse let me know that it was OK for me to use the bathroom in his room, since I was staying over. She also arranged for a guest mattress to be delivered. It was much more comfortable than the fold-out chair bed in the ICU.

In the wee hours of that night, on the guest mattress in Dennis's hospital room, on the fifth floor of the tower on the Cherry Hill campus of Swedish Medical Center, was my first chance to breathe since Dennis had first mentioned two weeks earlier that he'd been *feeling a little dizzy lately.*

My first chance to ponder and reflect. My first chance to let sink in what was going on around me.

My world had suddenly shrunk to the four walls of my home and the four walls of the hospital, and I had no idea what was in store for us in the ensuing eight months.

Nor in the rest of my life that would follow.

If I'd had any inkling of what was to come, I'd have been asking myself.

Can I really handle this?

5

Saturday
May 16, 2015

Dennis slept well and made some small steps
forward with OT today. However, much uphill
battle appears to remain. Please continue your
prayers and best thoughts. I am home, and
taking the kids back to see him this evening
at his request.

Thank you so much to everyone who has been at
the house and helping in every other way. Many
might not know that we were in the middle of
an unplanned kitchen remodel, so everything
has been a disaster at the house.

Another just-the-facts update. It would take a while before I would get into a more reflective frame of mind when updating CaringBridge.

Before I began to find my voice.

For now, I was in can-do mode, dealing with the day-to-day tasks required of the spouse of a person who has just had a craniotomy—a fancy word I learned for "your skull was cut open."

Physical therapists dropped by the room. Occupational therapists. Speech therapists. His speech was fine—but, as I learned, speech therapists also address cognitive issues.

Which he had—no doubt about it.

During one of the early visits from Speech (meaning the speech therapy team), the therapist administered some sort of assessment. She asked questions such as: "*Which is bigger: a horse or a dog?*"

He was stumped.

Her other questions were similarly baffling.

He might have post-operative swelling, she said. *This might be temporary.*

It wasn't.

As I'd later learn, glioblastoma is insidious like that. It spreads quickly and can spring up from a few cells to a full-fledged tumor that impacts daily living in a matter of weeks. Depending on where it is in the brain, those impacts can show up very differently. In Dennis's case, it affected him cognitively.

It was his *slight* dizziness—and *slight* confusion—that concerned me in the first place. That his cognitive issues increased dramatically over a ten-day period is what led me to call his doctor and advocate for him to be seen right away. By the time of his first surgery, he was confused enough that he botched the instructions for the special pre-surgery shampoo—

but not so much that he didn't have *some* moments where he seemed his usual self.

That first surgery changed everything. He was, quite literally, never the same again. It was as if I lost my husband for the first time that day—before losing him again eight months later.

At this point, I'd stayed overnight at the hospital for two nights. I hadn't seen the kids since we dropped them off at school on Thursday morning on the way to Dennis's surgery. They were safe and cared for—staying with family—but the preceding couple of days had been very disruptive for them. Scary. They knew that their dad had a brain tumor—that's all any of us knew at that point. And I hadn't been there to help them process any of it.

Not that I'd have known what to say.

On this day, Dennis asked to see the kids, so I agreed to bring them for a visit that evening. I thought he might be in the hospital for a week or more, so bringing Peter and Megan to see him seemed a good idea. As I drove back across the lake, toward home, I wondered: *Should I stay at the hospital again tonight, or should I stay at home? Am I needed on the medical front, or do the kids need time at home, with me?*

I didn't know what was the "right" answer.

Nor did I know the answers to many other questions swirling around in my head:

How much should I tell the kids about Dennis's illness?

Should they visit him in the hospital if he's appearing unwell?

What do I say if they ask how serious it is?

To make matters worse, I didn't even know who could guide me on this journey. I felt completely and utterly lost.

Most of all, I wanted to know: *how do I parent through this health crisis that may not have a happy ending?*

6

_____

Sunday
May 17, 2015

Not much change or new info today. Dennis
remained stable, had some visitors, and
rested. He watched the Mariners. I think the
coming days will bring more information and
clarity on next steps.

On the home front, some wonderfully angelic
people came today, the result of which is that
we now have the sink, stove, dishwasher, and
microwave in place. Wow. So appreciate it.

_____

L ittle did I know that watching the Mariners would become
a lifeline in the ensuing months.
You see, there are a lot of hours to fill when someone is in
the hospital. Sure, there are visits from physical therapy (PT),

occupational therapy (OT), and speech therapy (Speech). (Why that doesn't get abbreviated, like "PT" and "OT," I'll never know.) Nurses come by to monitor vitals, and they bring medication every few hours. Sometimes doctors stop in. But mostly, it's a lot of sit-around-and-do-nothing for the patient and visitors.

It's not like we were able to use that time in any constructive ways. There was no "let's have meaningful conversations" or "let's plan bucket list activities" or "let's tackle something important," like having Dennis write his life story for the kids to read someday. The cancer cells embedded in his brain made any of those activities impossible.

Enter Major League Baseball.

The beautiful thing is, the Mariners play practically every day during the season. At home or on the road, it's going to be on television. Enjoying the game doesn't require keeping up a conversation, nor does it require the complex thinking of, say, some board games. Even better, it takes *many hours* to play a game. Hours that needed to be filled.

It's a perfect hospital-room pastime.

Sometimes, while watching the game, my mind would wander. It would jump ahead, to ponder what my life would look like in the future. What my kids' lives would look like.

Later that summer, taking in our gazillionth Mariners game of the season, there would be a special pre-game presentation that caught my attention. Former Mariner Jamie Moyer—a star pitcher on the team in Dennis's and my early adult years in Seattle—was being inducted into the Mariners Hall of Fame.

When the presenter began to speak about Moyer's community contributions, I could hardly believe my ears. Together with Karen Phelps Moyer, he had founded what was then the Moyer Foundation (now Eluna)—which included a nationwide network of children's grief camps called Camp Erin. These were camps specifically for kids who had lost a parent or sibling.

I didn't even know that such a thing existed.

As I sat there in the visitor chair in the hospital—next to my terminally ill husband—I had just one thought: *I have to write this down. One day, this will be important.*

I was not a therapist. Or a parenting expert. I didn't have a degree in psychology, or in child development.

I was a corporate IT person. A project manager. And a competent-enough parent, to be sure—but so far, my parenting experience was limited to run-of-the-mill childhood issues.

But this—this was a whole new ball game.

And I was racked with doubt: could I possibly learn to navigate this traumatic experience in my kids' young lives in such a way that they could go on to become whole and healthy adults?

I had no choice—I was about to find out.

7

Monday
May 18, 2015

```
Today seems a quiet day. Visits from various
therapists. Visitors. Seems likely Dennis will
transfer to inpatient rehab tomorrow. Kids
will be here soon to visit again, which will
be good for all.
```

O n this day, the kids were coming back to the hospital. I can't say for sure, but this may have been the time they arrived and I went to the lobby to tell them they couldn't see their dad.

Which was a disaster.

I was at the hospital every day, and always for several hours or more, but not overnight after those first two nights. Peter and Megan liked to visit Dennis, but there wasn't much for them to do there. Their tolerance for sitting around a hospital was much less than mine, so their visits were generally much shorter. Often the kids stayed with family or friends when I was at the hospital. On days they would visit, the plan was typically either for them to go with me and be picked up by someone after an hour or two, or for them to be dropped off midway through my visit, after which they'd come home with me.

One day early in Dennis's illness—perhaps this day—I was at the hospital for some hours and expecting the kids to come see him after school. But—he was more confused than usual. And they hadn't witnessed him in this state yet.

I didn't know what to do. *Should they see him like this? Was it better to somehow shield them from it?*

Like parents everywhere, I wanted to protect my kids. The problem was, I didn't know what "protecting them" meant in this situation.

Grandma and Grandpa texted to say they had arrived in the hospital lobby, and I made my way down. I don't remember what I told the kids, but the gist of it was *you can't see Dad right now, even though you just came all the way to the hospital to do exactly that.* I was afraid to tell them why.

Like I said before—disaster ensued. Meltdowns. Crying. Anger.

What I know now—that I didn't know then—is that my approach likely scared them. They were expecting to see their dad, and all of a sudden, without explanation, the plan had changed. Now Mom was saying they couldn't. They probably concocted a story in their minds about his condition that was much worse than the truth, I'd later learn. And that image may have traumatized them.

But I don't know what they thought or felt. I never asked them.

I wish I had.

. . .

What I also didn't know then is that one in fourteen kids will experience the death of a parent or sibling before they turn eighteen.

One in fourteen.

I had no idea that childhood grief was so prevalent.

You see, I didn't really know anyone close to me who had died, until I lost my grandma—when I was in my mid-twenties. I couldn't think of any friends or classmates from my childhood who had lost parents. I knew, of course, that it was theoretically possible—but it seemed just that: a remote possibility. Not something that would happen to me, or to anyone I knew.

Certainly not to *my kids*.

Losing a parent in childhood is one of the so-called "Adverse Childhood Experiences"—ACEs—that can wreak havoc in a young life. The more ACEs a child endures, the greater their risk of physical and emotional struggles in adulthood.

But here's the thing: *every child deserves a chance to thrive.*

How ever would my kids get that chance?

8

Messages for Dennis
May 18, 2015

Dennis is starting to grasp why he is in the
hospital, and I think he might be ready to
enjoy some messages from family and friends.
If anyone wants to post a message, or send me
one, I'll be sure to read it to him in the
coming days.

Thanks so much for all the continued support.

———

By this time, we were eighteen days into the journey.
Eighteen days since Dennis said *I've been feeling a little
dizzy lately.*

It felt like eighteen *months* already.

Perhaps I exaggerate.

But truly, our lives had turned inward and upside down in a

matter of weeks. I now had a pinball-like existence, bouncing back and forth between the hospital and our home. In the coming months, we'd add a skilled nursing facility and a couple other clinics at Swedish into the rotation—radiation oncology and infectious disease, primarily—but my world got very narrow, and it did so almost overnight.

Our new existence was a drastic departure from what had been *normal* just weeks before.

Dennis and I had both worked full time. He loved his job as a city planner, working at City Hall in Redmond—the Seattle suburb in which we lived.

I had, at that point, been at a large tech company for sixteen years, and had been working remotely for the past twelve. I worked with a New York-based team, so as I said, I started early —around 6:00 a.m.—and finished in time to pick the kids up from school. My schedule allowed me to integrate motherhood and career—and I made it work, despite my night-owl tendencies.

We were also tied up with activities typical of a family with two grade-school-aged kids—recreational sports most seasons, Boy Scouts and Girl Scouts, friend sleepovers, family trips, and the like. Throw in a dog and a cat, and a home to care for, and our lives were full.

Now that my participation in anything resembling normal life had screeched to a halt, I assigned myself the task of coordinating messages for my hospitalized husband.

Which, at the time, seemed like such a big accomplishment.

9

Transforred to rehab unit
May 19, 2015

Today Dennis was transferred to inpatient
rehab. Not much to report so far. We've been
getting acclimated, and I got a tour. He is
napping now. Tomorrow they will develop a
treatment plan and daily schedule. He does
seem improved today. Tomorrow we meet with the
oncologist.

By the way, if anyone wants to post or send a
message for Dennis, don't feel it needs to be
lengthy or profound.

I'm sure a brief greeting and well wishes
would be just fine. :)

One of the things you learn quickly when facing a serious illness is that some people just kind of "get it." They aren't afraid to talk about difficult things, and aren't afraid of interacting with you. Others—maybe most, actually—can be quite uncomfortable. Many people just don't know what to say.

Sometimes, I noticed, people would not say anything at all. Perhaps they were afraid of saying the wrong thing. I get where they were coming from; I've made this mistake plenty of times myself.

I don't know what to say. I don't know the right words to make this better. I want to fix this, but don't know how. Maybe it's not any of my business anyway. Maybe I'll magically think of the right thing to say in the future, so I'll wait until then to say something.

The thing is, no one can say just the right thing to fix it. This is because nothing actually *can* fix it—certainly not words—and sometimes trying to say something profound just makes the situation worse. It might leave the listener feeling that the well-wisher doesn't "get it." Or worse, it may invalidate their experience.

Saying nothing at all makes it worse, too. Saying nothing makes the person think: *Why haven't I heard from this friend? Do they care? Do they even know?*

As it turns out, no profound remarks are required. The simplest message—I'm here, and I care—is all that's needed.

Even at this early stage of our journey, I recognized that I could use the posts I was writing to coach others on how to be good allies to those in pain or grief. At the very least, by being open about our situation and experiences, I could help them feel more comfortable interacting with us.

Which was, of course, helpful for me, too—because dealing with other people's discomfort was an additional burden I couldn't handle.

10

Update
May 20, 2015

Dennis has been diagnosed with aggressive brain cancer: grade 4 glioblastoma.

Radiation and chemo will start in about a week.

B y now it had been just six days since Dennis's first surgery. Not quite three weeks since his first symptoms. I felt like he'd been in the hospital—like we'd been in this ordeal —forever.

Dennis was staying in the inpatient rehab unit at Swedish, so for his appointment with the neuro-oncologist, I had to get him from his room and transport him in a wheelchair to the Ivy Center's office in the adjacent tower. This was the first of many times I'd take a similar trip, from his room on one end of campus to the neurosurgeon's and oncologist's office on the other end. Dennis was generally unaware of the gravity of his situation, and I was in can-do mode; there was little time to stop and reflect on just how surreal day-to-day life had become.

The meeting with the oncologist that day was an important one. The biopsy results were back, and this was our first chance to hear any definitive information.

"It's cancer," she said to Dennis and me, and to our parents, all assembled in the small exam room.

It was the news we'd been dreading.

Not only that, she explained, the neurosurgeon had only been able to get enough of the tumor to do a biopsy. He hadn't "removed" much of it at all. It wasn't a discrete tumor that could be cut around and removed; instead, cancer cells were woven throughout the fabric of his brain.

Specifically, Dennis was diagnosed with glioblastoma. It's a terrible disease that, at the time, had just killed Beau Biden, son of then-Vice President Joe Biden. As we'd learned from Google the night before Dennis's first surgery, the survival rate is generally poor.

Which is probably an understatement.

"What is the prognosis?" I asked the doctor.

She asked Dennis if he wanted to know. He didn't. We stepped into another room, and she shared the verdict with me.

"I can't tell you what it will be in his case, but the average life expectancy is thirteen months," she said.

Somehow, I knew in my gut we'd be lucky if he got that much time.

Up until this point, I hadn't known for sure what we were dealing with.

Now it was impossible to deceive myself.

From the beginning, it was *thought* to be bad. Serious. Maybe even life-threatening.

But—I didn't *know* that.

Until the diagnosis of glioblastoma, all we knew was that Dennis had a *brain tumor*. I could hope that he might have the type that was fixable. I could imagine that clinical trials might be in our future. I could think in terms of *fighting cancer* or maybe even *beating cancer*. Perhaps the tumor would even turn out to be benign. At the very least, it was not unreasonable to be holding out hope in those early days.

With this diagnosis of glioblastoma, everything changed. We would of course pursue the standard of care—chemotherapy and radiation—because in situations like this, you try those things that might work. Even glioblastoma's five-year survival rate in the single digits meant that a *few* people would make it.

But, as I soon learned, the options available to us were very limited, and not likely to fix anything.

And so, with this diagnosis, my role shifted. Barring some type of miracle, I would accompany my husband through his terminal cancer, and be his full-time caregiver for his remaining days.

Now it fell to me to break the news to Peter and Megan. I was at a total loss as to what I should tell them, and when.

And I didn't even know who could answer that for me.

The problem is, Dennis's diagnosis was public knowledge already. I'd shared it on CaringBridge, and the principal at their school, St. Louise, had updated the entire school community (with my permission, of course).

One of my close friends called me that night and asked how —and when—I was planning to tell the kids. I told her I didn't know. She could probably tell that it was a conversation I was hoping to avoid altogether.

"You need to tell them the truth," she urged me. "And soon. We told our kids at dinner that Dennis had cancer, and they asked if he was going to die. I'm sure many parents are having the same conversation with their kids tonight. You don't want yours hearing about this on the playground tomorrow. They need to hear it from you, and they need to hear it tonight."

She was right, of course. Pushing me out of my comfort zone turned out to be a gift.

But—how do I even have this conversation at all—much less the "right" way?

I had no guidebook to tell me what to say—nor the time to find such a thing, if it even existed.

I gathered both kids in Megan's room and sat down cross-legged on the carpet with them on my lap. At eight and ten, they didn't fit easily, but it seemed the thing to do.

"Guys," I started. "We saw the doctor today. Dad's tumor is cancer. The doctors said they can't fix it."

"Is he going to live to see me graduate?" asked Megan. At that point, her high school graduation was still a decade away.

"No, honey, he won't," I said softly, through the tears.

"Will he live until Christmas?" At eight, Christmas seemed a big milestone on the calendar.

"I don't know. I sure hope so."

Peter heard my voice shaking and whipped around to look at my face. "I didn't know adults cried," he said, with a look of alarm on his face.

This would mark the first of many difficult discussions in my new role as a future-widowed-parent. Because for all practical purposes, I was now the kids' only parent. I was definitely the only one able to do any parenting.

And I still had no idea what I was doing.

11

Friday & Saturday
May 23, 2015

Some more wonderfully angelic people were at
our house last night. Lots of them. I am overwhelmed by all the kindness, generosity, and
effort. The house and yard look fabulous.
People came bearing food, drink, paintbrushes,
and shovels. And everything looks so great.
Really, thank you all so much. As someone
said, HGTV has nothing on this group!

Today Dennis enjoyed some visitors and lots of
therapy sessions. Megan and I were there when
PT came, and accompanied him on an outside
walk. He enjoyed that. He seems to be stable,
and is working hard on therapy goals so he can
come home.

I mentioned to him that we had a CaringBridge

site setup so people could keep up to date
with his situation. I asked him how many visitors he thought the site had. He guessed maybe
25 or 30--and couldn't believe it when I told
him there had been over 1,000 hits at the
time.

Peter is away camping with his Boy Scout
troop, and Megan enjoyed some time at a
friend's house last night and today. I slept
in this morning, and have been trying to hold
down the fort. Thanks so much to everyone
helping me do so.

———

I remember so clearly coming back to my house on this
particular Friday evening, just eight days after Dennis's first
surgery. By then it seemed like he had been at the hospital for
ages.

I mean, we'd already been through brain surgery, a night in
ICU, some nights on the regular floor, and now he was well-integrated into the routine at the inpatient rehab unit. All just
different floors in the same place. Same drive for me across Lake
Washington, fighting traffic on Interstate 90. Same parking
garage, same skybridge into the building. Same Starbucks in the
lobby.

Same. Same. Same. Day in and day out.

On this particular evening, I took a break from hanging out
in the hospital room to buzz home and check on the work party
happening at our house. When Dennis went into primary care
for his very first visit, we actually left the flooring contractor at
our house finishing up installation of the kitchen and living

room floor. We had no sink, stove, dishwasher, or microwave. The refrigerator was plugged in on the back deck, and the barbecue—fortunately with a side burner—was our only way to cook. We'd had significant water damage in the kitchen leading to a near gutting of the room—and I was acting as general contractor on the effort to restore the house to working order. The project couldn't have come at a worse time.

Word of our kitchen predicament got out pretty quickly among the St. Louise school community, and soon I was asked for a "brain dump" on the status of open items for the kitchen project. A couple of the parents in Megan's class spearheaded a work party to get our house livable before Dennis came home. After all, we would need an oven to heat up the casseroles that would be coming via the meal train that yet another parent had set up.

When I arrived home that evening, I was amazed how many people were there working on the house. In the front yard, friends were weeding, trimming, edging, and spreading bark. Someone was blowing debris off the roof. Inside, more friends were painting walls, ceilings, and trim. Someone installed the new doorbell. The stove, sink, dishwasher, and refrigerator were hooked up. I made my way to the backyard, where I witnessed more cleanup in progress. Others supplied food and beverages to keep the group going.

I'm sure I'm forgetting some of the tasks on the list, but suffice it to say, a large group can get a lot done in an evening. It transformed our kitchen space—and more.

These days when I am doing yardwork, I can still see the folks who were out there pulling weeds that evening. I can still see my neighbor on a stool in my dining room, covering the ceiling with a fresh layer of paint. I can still tap into the feeling I had as I visited with each and every person there.

I was so very glad they had rallied to come out that evening and prepare our home for Dennis's return. We'd been limping along with a mix of takeout and meals cooked via barbecue, one burner, and an ancient, borrowed countertop microwave. We'd managed satisfactorily before Dennis became ill; afterwards, it would have been next to impossible.

The funny thing is, I got the sense that the people there that night were glad they'd come, too. One thing I've learned in this journey is that everyone wants to help. What everyone desires most is not only to *say something* to fix it, but to *do something* to fix it. Whatever "it" is—take away the cancer, take away the terminal diagnosis. The thing is, they can't. But what they *can* do is cook, build, paint, and pull weeds. They can shop, carpool kids, walk dogs, and take out the trash. They could ease my burden by taking practical, tangible tasks off my plate.

And that meant the world to me.

12

Sunday

May 24, 2015

Big news--Dennis will likely be coming home on Tuesday!

Today I was there during an OT session when he went to their kitchen to make scrambled eggs. He also got outside again today with PT. He is looking forward to coming home.

———

This post sounded so hopeful: *he made eggs with the occupational therapist today.* In reality, watching Dennis make breakfast in the OT kitchen was anything but.

I learned that when you work with a therapist, they need to set official goals. It's part of how the medical system works. The doctor makes a referral for PT or OT—or in Dennis's case, both of those, plus Speech. Then the therapist does an assessment. And sets goals.

PT wants to know what your house is like, so they can set appropriate goals for going home. How many stairs do you have? Do you have a shower or bathtub, and what physical skills or strengthening do they need to work on so you can use it? OT creates goals for things like being able to fix yourself breakfast.

I'm not sure how this whole process is supposed to work if you don't have family caring for you who can make plans with the therapists.

For many years, Dennis was the primary cook in our family. When we lived in Yonkers, New York—with both of us working, and no kids yet—he tended to cook most of our meals. He actually liked it, and he enjoyed finding new recipes in *The New York Times* or one of our (read: *his*) many cookbooks.

Once we moved to Portland, Oregon, and I was working East Coast hours, I became the "weekday cook," and he was the "weekend cook." We switched up from time to time, depending primarily on scheduling considerations. Mostly, though, he loved to prepare meals for our family, and I didn't.

So, when the therapist raised the topic of OT goals, it made sense to target something around cooking. We talked about how Dennis liked to cook, and especially how he liked to make eggs. In fact, he had taught me to make eggs. (I don't especially like eggs, which is why I never bothered to learn.) He also had taught Megan to make eggs. It seemed a good goal for him to be able to make eggs again himself. He would enjoy this activity, and it would give him a sense of purpose at home.

It would also buy us a small slice of normal, in the very abnormal world we were inhabiting.

That's how we settled on "making scrambled eggs" as an official goal of OT. So, this particular Sunday found us in the OT kitchen of the rehab unit at Swedish. I stood back and observed while the therapist coached him through the process.

"What equipment do you need to make scrambled eggs?"

"What ingredients?"

"Where would you find the eggs?"

Watching from my position off to the side, I had a sinking feeling: *this is going to be a disaster.* Most of the questions stumped him, and he required a lot of coaching to identify that he needed a pan, bowl, fork, wooden spoon, etc. He didn't say much. But once he had the equipment and ingredients in front of him, he whipped up the eggs without issue. Muscle memory kicked in.

At home, this goal quickly fell apart. It just wasn't safe for him to be using the kitchen by himself. Case in point: one Sunday morning around 5:00 a.m., I woke to find him standing next to my side of the bed.

"I can't get the stove turned on."

He was standing there, fully dressed for work—shoes on and City of Redmond employee badge in his pocket—and gently waking me.

What the hell????

I flew out of bed and down the stairs. I smelled something burning on the way down.

When I got to the kitchen, I found that he had been trying to make breakfast. He had the equipment and ingredients. He had eggs scrambled in a bowl. Getting the gas burner going had stumped him.

The oven was on—which explained the charred smell. It must have been the residue of some prior spill—something I'd been too busy to deal with. He hadn't put anything in the oven. So, fortunately, nothing was actually on fire.

That was the day I ordered safety covers for the knobs on the stove, and it was the end of "cooking" as a goal for OT.

13

Home
May 27, 2015

Dennis came home last night. We are all glad
to have him home. He seems in good spirits,
though tired.

Today was the first radiation treatment. It
was quick. He will be going every day for
that. Swedish hospital in Issaquah is a nice
place--pretty convenient, and such caring
staff. We also had a nice visit to St. Louise
when we dropped the kids off at school this
morning.

Thanks to all for the continued support in so
many ways, including such yummy food. We
appreciate it so much.

I noted above that we had a nice visit to St. Louise that day. And we did. But—these visits were always a bit of a double-edged sword.

If you had to read *The Scarlet Letter* in high school, you probably remember Hester Prynne. She was sentenced to wear a big, red letter "A"—for Adultery—on her chest as penance for her crime, making her status easily identifiable by all.

Well, I have to tell you, for the duration of Dennis's illness, I felt like Hester Prynne. I had the overwhelming sense I was walking around with a giant "FW" emblazoned on my shirt.

Future Widow.

I especially felt this when walking around the kids' school. St. Louise has a wonderful, tight-knit, caring community. And it seemed like just about everyone there—those I knew, and those I didn't—had heard about our situation.

Many people at the school, and elsewhere, were following my posts on CaringBridge. That was fine with me—I'd rather be open about it, so people would know what was happening, and so neither I nor anyone else would be dancing around the topic. This approach of sharing openly also resulted in a tremendous amount of support for my family, which I very much appreciated. And very much needed.

There was a downside, however. I could not walk around the kids' school without feeling like all eyes were on me. I imagined they were thinking, *oh, there's that poor woman again.*

And: *she's a future widow.*

Maybe I was overthinking it. Maybe I was assuming that everyone was following along more closely than they actually were. Maybe I figured that people would know that "glioblastoma" may as well have been synonymous with "death sentence"—or do a quick web search if they didn't. I had posted about Dennis's diagnosis in a "just the facts" manner—without elaboration, or editorial comment—as I didn't have the where-withal to do anything else. Anyway, when you're deep in the middle of a crisis, it can be hard to have proper perspective on what others may be thinking.

I do know that the question "how *are* you?"—which was, of course, asked when I ran into just about anyone—would usually throw me into an existential tailspin.

It seems like a simple question. Uttered, often, without thought. A greeting, almost, in normal circumstances.

"Hey, how are you?"

"Fine, how are you?"

"Fine, thanks."

And then everyone goes about their day.

Except, when your forty-four-year-old husband has brain cancer, it's not such a simple question.

The inquiry might come at school pickup. It might come by text; it might come from a neighbor or friend stopping by with dinner; it might come on the sidelines of the soccer field.

Getting this question—which, I should add, was always coming from someone sincere and well-meaning—would cause fits of uncertainty in me.

You see, I find it an impossible question. It requires a series of split-second calculations:

Who is asking? Do they really want to know, or are they just being polite?

How much do they already know? If I were to even begin to answer, how much context do I need to give? Are they interested in summary-level status, or the details of the latest medical news?

Am I even interested in telling this person how I really and truly am?

And anyway, how am I? Can I even answer that for myself, much less for anyone else?

At any given moment, there might be multiple answers that

were all true. I mean, on one level, I might be fine. Or even good. I might not have a headache, and I might have eaten recently, for example. But on another level—say, the existential level—my whole life was falling apart before my eyes. So, in that respect, I was the exact opposite of "fine."

More often than not, all these thoughts would swirl in my head for a fraction of a second, I'd sigh and give up, and out of my mouth would come: "fine." Which was neither helpful nor accurate, but it was all I could muster. And I'd miss a chance to connect with someone who really did care, and really did want to help.

I learned from this experience that "how are you *today*" is a more manageable question than the all-encompassing "how are you?" It narrows the question down to one I'm much more likely to be able to answer. These days, I try to keep this in mind when checking on friends who are grieving or struggling in some way. I don't always remember, but I always hope to.

14

Working on a "new normal"
May 30, 2015

Dennis has been home for a few days now, and
we are all adjusting. He seems to enjoy being
here, and we are glad he is.

Being home isn't always easy, however, because
of significant short-term memory issues caused
by the location of the tumor. Dennis has the
skills to do lots of things, but needs a lot
of cueing and supervision for safety reasons.
He also is having issues with what they call
"orientation"--such as waking up in the middle
of the night and thinking it's time to get up,
dressed, etc. PT and Speech have been
prescribed in order to work on these areas.
Radiation and chemo are underway--so far no
adverse effects.

Today, Dennis (and Peter) got haircuts. It's a big improvement. :) Tomorrow we are going to see the Mariners, at Dennis's request. We are all looking forward to that outing with my sister's family. Kids apparently get to go on the field prior to the start of the game since it's Little League day.

Some St. Louise folks came over and said a lovely Rosary a couple of nights ago. Dennis decided he did want to join the group in our front yard, and said he enjoyed it. He also enjoyed spending the day with his mom yesterday.

Kids are doing so well with Dennis. They have been so helpful and encouraging with him. Then they are sad later.

I could not hold down the fort and deal with all the paperwork, logistics, and decisions without the help of so many. Thank you, again.

I'm sure I'm forgetting some things, but that is the gist of it. Thanks everyone, too, for your messages and cards. They mean so much.

———

R eading this post now, five years later, gives me a sense of just how slow time was for us while Dennis was sick. This was about two-and-a-half weeks after his first surgery, and here I was talking about establishing a "new normal." I want to reach back in time and tell myself: *just wait—the worst is still ahead of you.*

At the time, I was deep into this new reality. I mean, a few weeks immersed in the world of a brain cancer patient feels like a whole lifetime's worth of medical encounters.

I clearly remember taking Dennis for this haircut. It had been a while since he'd had it cut, and his hair was getting pretty long. Hair was also falling out in the areas where the radiation was focused, and his head still bore the marks of the brain surgery he'd had two weeks earlier. The combination of these factors meant that he was desperately in need of a haircut.

I still remember the look on his barber's face when we walked in. He had been cutting Dennis's hair for years, and Dennis always looked forward to catching up when he went in every month or so. On this particular day, Dennis walked in looking like he'd aged a decade or more since his last visit. He was weak and pale, and looked very much like someone who had been hospitalized for several weeks. He was also unsteady on his feet, and was wearing a "gait belt"—a thick woven strap worn over the clothes which gives the therapist or caregiver something to hold onto to prevent falls.

The barber took one look at him and looked like he'd seen a ghost. The shock on his face was palpable. He waved Dennis over to the chair right away, and looked at me as if to say *what the hell is going on?*

I pulled him aside. "It's cancer," I said. "Brain cancer."

"Can the doctors do anything?"

"The prognosis is bad. Really, really bad."

He wiped away tears and turned to Dennis, and started his last real haircut.

15

Article: **Brain cancers like Beau Biden's kill about 15,000 adults each year**
May 31, 2015

It's suspected that Beau Biden may have had the same type of cancer Dennis has.

Link to Washington Post article:
bit.ly/beau-biden-article

This particular day on CaringBridge, I shared an article that I thought had a good summary of what glioblastoma was, and the fact that the prognosis was bleak.

Beau Biden, son of then-Vice President Joe Biden, was admitted to the hospital a few days after Dennis's first surgery with a diagnosis of terminal brain cancer. He died about 10 days later. For this reason, glioblastoma was all over the news in those early days and weeks of our ordeal. I think some of those close to me were hoping I wouldn't see these news accounts, but they were unavoidable. And of course, I sought out every article I could find on the topic. The specific type of brain cancer that Biden had was not immediately released, but all signs pointed to glioblastoma—the same type Dennis had.

When I shared this article on CaringBridge, I didn't have the energy to add any comments around it. The facts would have to stand alone, and convey their message themselves.

16

Events of the past few days
June 2, 2015

Late last night Dennis was quite uncomfortable (full bladder) so we went to the ER. We returned home with a catheter in place. Next steps TBD.

In in other news, the Mariners game was great. Dennis enjoyed it and wanted to stay the entire game (including extra innings). Wheelchair service by the stadium guest services staff was so helpful.

I have been dealing with paperwork and other such exciting things in between all the other.

Hopefully all the news around Beau Biden will raise awareness of glioblastoma and result in some breakthroughs that will someday help someone. Part of Dennis's tumor has already gone into the research pipeline.

A h, the Mariners game. I summarized it originally as "great," and in some respects, it was. It was our first big outing of any type, and it was logistically successful. A family friend had arranged close-in parking and wheelchair service for us, and that turned out to be extremely helpful. At the time, Dennis was not entirely wheelchair-bound, but a visit to a major league ballpark can involve a lot of walking, and he was in no condition to tackle that.

Most importantly, Dennis enjoyed it. He always loved the Mariners, and over the years had proudly told me how he and his buddies used to get tickets in the "cheap seats" way back when the Kingdome was still around. I think this was probably when he was in high school.

This particular game was very long. The kids and I probably would have been just as happy packing it in early, but Dennis wanted to stay for the entire game. By halfway through, I had to step out. I left our seats—my sister and family were there to keep an eye on things—and made my way out to the concourse. As I stood near the bathrooms, tears began to flow—and I couldn't shake the very real sense that this was almost certainly Dennis's last Mariners game.

By then I just wanted to get out of there, and was mentally counting down to the ninth inning. I put my sunglasses on and made my way back to the seats, red eyes covered. When I see pictures from that day, I can see how tired I looked. Already. Still only a month into what would turn out to be an eight-month journey.

By the end of the ninth inning, the game was tied. Dennis

wanted to stay. Not one—not two—but *three* more innings went by before the visiting team finally scored three more runs and won the game. I would have gladly left before that point, but there was no way I'd pull Dennis away from his last baseball game. Ever.

This was the first time I had a real gut-level sense that some activity or event would most likely be Dennis's last. It was a surreal—and sickening—feeling, being conscious that the things we were planning and doing would probably be his last times to do them.

Especially when he didn't—couldn't—have the awareness of this fact.

17

Sheryl Sandberg on grief
June 5, 2015

Sheryl Sandberg, COO of Facebook, lost her husband suddenly and unexpectedly about a month ago. Yesterday she wrote this excellent post on grief: bit.ly/sandberg-post-grief

We continue to go day by day here. Dennis has had some increased nursing needs this week, which we got through. He is tired, but enjoying puzzles, cooking shows, and short dog walks. Daily radiation and medication continue. Thank you, everyone, for the continued support, both logistical and emotional.

One thing I seemed to have time for—with all those hours sitting around the hospital, or sitting up at night while everyone else was asleep—was scrolling through my phone. I continued to keep a very close eye on Sheryl Sandberg's Facebook posts, as I knew in my gut that I would soon be following in her footsteps as a young widow. Her kids were even in the same ballpark, age-wise, as my kids.

Her post on grief to mark the end of the formal thirty-day grieving period in her Jewish faith was phenomenal. Looking back at the above post now, I think I understated its importance. I said at the time that it was an "excellent post." I wish I'd said, "EVERYONE PLEASE GO READ THIS RIGHT NOW." My intention in sharing it was to let her words give my community a window into grief in a way that I could not yet articulate.

Re-reading it now, I'm struck by Sheryl's openness and vulnerability in sharing her journey with—quite literally—the whole world. She's one of the tech industry's most powerful people, and she let us in. She helped us understand what it's like to go back to work when there's a gigantic elephant in the room, and your colleagues don't know what to say to you. She brought us into her home, sharing with us how her mother tried to fill the void in her bed by holding her every night until she cried herself to sleep. She confessed that she'd done everything exactly wrong in the past when trying to support others in their times of need. She suggested ways to do better.

Her post ends by relating a story that would become the genesis of her later grief work, including her book with Wharton professor Adam Grant, *Option B: Facing Adversity, Building Resilience, and Finding Joy*.

She writes: "I was talking to [a friend] about a father-child activity that Dave is not here to do. We came up with a plan to fill in for Dave. I cried to him, 'But I want Dave. I want option A.'

He put his arm around me and said, 'Option A is not available. So let's just kick the shit out of Option B.'"

Most of all, I love this sentiment she shares:

"A childhood friend of mine who is now a rabbi recently told me that the most powerful one-line prayer he has ever read is: 'Let me not die while I am still alive.' I would have never understood that prayer before losing Dave. Now I do."

Let me not die while I am still alive. Such a powerful idea. This is one of the early breadcrumbs that I was finding along the way, helping me shape my thinking about my path ahead, and helping me to find my way forward.

I continued to follow Sheryl's grief-related work closely. I read every post she wrote about grief and loss. I watched the commencement address she gave a year later, where she spoke publicly for the first time since her husband's death. I read every article I could find, and read the book *Option B* as soon as it came out.

In fact, I'd followed her journey so closely that I was able to anticipate her remarks when I later went to see her speak in Seattle, along with Adam Grant, on their book tour. From my aisle seat in the seventh row, I jumped up when they announced they were going to take questions, got to the microphone first, and asked the very first question that night. I took a deep breath —there were probably 1,500 people in attendance at the beautiful, historic theater—and asked: "My kids are around the same age as your kids, and my husband died a year ago. What tips or suggestions do you have for parenting grieving kids?"

I asked this because I'd already absorbed the key points Sheryl shared about her own grief process. I wanted to know how she was helping her kids—because this had been top-of-mind for me from the beginning, and I wasn't finding any good answers out there.

18

ER again today
June 6, 2015

I'm writing this from the pharmacy, as I wait
for an oxycodone prescription to be filled for
Dennis's severe headache. Apparently, since
it's a controlled substance, the soonest they
can give it to me is 15 minutes--and this
after already trying two other pharmacies,
only to find that the pharmacist leaves at
6:00 on Saturdays.

The headache seems to be due to a fall earlier
today, where he hit mostly his back, but also
his head. The doctor said to take him to ER
for another CT scan. Results of that were
good--no bleeding. However, he does apparently
have a concussion. He was more confused and
unstable on his feet tonight, and now has this

headache. Hopefully the 15-minute waiting
period ends soon.

Today I couldn't help but think of two quotes:

"The best laid plans of mice and men / gang
aft aglay."

—Robert Burns, "To A Mouse," the poem from
which the Steinbeck book *Of Mice and Men* got
its name. (According to my recollection of
high school English--not my favorite subject--
the latter part is Old English or something,
and translates to "often go astray.")

"Whatever rug you are standing on can be
pulled right out from under you with absolutely no warning."

—Sheryl Sandberg, from her post on grief that
I reposted yesterday

This was not supposed to be our life. Yet we
go on, one day at a time.

Tomorrow the kids are going on an all-day
outing with family. I think we will watch
movies all day. Which really probably means we
will doze on the couch all day. Which will be
good. For both of us.

I remember how tired I was at this point. And to think, we weren't even a month into the journey. We'd already had enough surgeries, hospital stays, ER visits, medications, and issues to last a lifetime.

There was so much yet to come.

With this post, I can see a shift in my writing. Until this point, my posts had primarily been informational—relaying updates on Dennis's condition, and relating our comings and goings.

Now, I can see I was finally starting to hit my stride, and my voice was beginning to emerge. I was increasingly reflecting on our journey as we lived it. I was stealing quiet moments—such as on solo drives to the hospital, or even ducking out of Dennis's room to stretch my legs and hit the lobby coffee shop—to turn over ideas in my head. Ideas that might end up in blog posts. I also began to treasure the times I would stay up late, after everyone else in the house was in bed and the house was quiet, to reflect on the day's events, and on our new reality. From my perch on the living room couch, I'd grab the laptop, and I would write.

There's a phenomenon known as "anticipatory grief," which is basically when you start grieving ahead of an actual death, in anticipation of it coming. The Ivy Center even had an Anticipatory Grief group that met monthly for caregivers of patients. The therapist there invited me to it several times, but I continually declined.

Finally, I asked, "So what is this group, kind of like a Future Widows Club?" I forget her exact reply, but what I took away was: "basically, yes."

Yeah... pretty sure that's not for me.

Why I felt this way, I can't say for sure. At that point, my days were consumed with holding everything together—or attempting to, anyway. I was in can-do mode, not grief-group mode. And honestly, at the time, I don't know if I could have handled hearing about other people's grief—which seemed a prerequisite for joining such a group.

It turned out that writing was how I filled that need. Considering what I wanted to share forced me to process and distill my thinking. It required me to wrestle with fact and emotion. It imposed a structure—blogging—that helped me stay accountable. And it gave me a venue for speaking to my corner of the world.

I had never been a journal writer as a child, or at any point in my life, actually. I really started writing in high school, and it was social studies papers that stood out as my strong point. I suppose I did well with English papers, too, but I disliked analyzing literature, and therefore didn't have a lot of interest in writing those essays. Social studies, though, I really sunk my teeth into. Somehow it seemed more real and relevant—and interesting—to me than the stories found in century-old novels.

This continued in college as I wrote many papers for my political science and economics classes. I got pretty good at banging out a three- to five-page piece the night before it was due. I enjoyed turning over ideas and phrases in my head, considering how to construct a coherent argument and relate my point. The best part was, when I re-read an essay in subsequent days, I was invariably still happy with what I'd written. I was satisfied with the structure and word choices—and most especially with how it came together into a cohesive piece of persuasive writing. I enjoyed expressing my points of view this way, and found that I was able to do so effectively.

I didn't do any writing to speak of for the next couple decades. Emails, sure. But getting back into writing on Caring-Bridge when Dennis was sick kind of felt like coming home. No, I wasn't constructing an argument for a political science paper—

but the process of reflecting on my current realities, and considering how to communicate about them through the written word, turned out to be much the same.

And, it's funny—the laptop, to which I had been chained for so many years of corporate work, was becoming my lifeline to the outside world. The four walls of our home and the hospital were small, but the audience I could reach with my writing was not.

19

No movies today--back at ER
June 7, 2015

It seems more plans are going astray. I guess
watching movies and sleeping were not meant to
be today.

Dennis's severe headache persisted, in spite
of oxycodone, and so we are back at ER today.
Been here several hours already; likely
several more before I go home. They are admit-
ting him overnight for observation and pain
meds. Lab work and today's CT scan looked
unchanged, which is good.

Thanks everyone for your kind messages. So
appreciate them.

So many ER visits. I've never been in the ER so many times in my entire life—before or since—as I was with Dennis while he was sick.

I remember the first time something happened outside office hours, I wasn't sure if I should take him to urgent care or the ER. And, if the ER, I wasn't sure if I should take him to the closer one in the suburbs, or the one downtown on the same campus as his neurosurgeon and oncologist. I guess I was used to "normal" considerations: go to the simplest place that will provide appropriate care. So, for example, possible strep throat: no need for the ER, urgent care will be just fine.

Pretty quickly I learned: always take him to the ER, and always take him downtown. Even if the traffic is bad, even if it's late at night and it's not in a great part of town. Because more often than not, he had to be admitted following one of these visits. And if he was going to be admitted, he needed to be at the Swedish Cherry Hill campus, where they had a neuro unit, and where his neurosurgeon could pop over to see him. Or where I could wheel him to the Ivy Center office.

I also learned that you can't just get someone admitted to the hospital unless there is an attending physician to admit them. So, for example, the nurse—or even the physician's assistant—in the Ivy Center couldn't admit him to the hospital if the neurosurgeon was away. But, I could call the Ivy Center, let them know what was happening, and ask for their direction. Often, they'd agree that he needed to be admitted, and tell me to take him to the ER to make that happen. Then they'd call down and tell the ER team that we were coming, brief them on the situation, and request that he be admitted straight to the fifth-floor neuro unit.

The first time this happened, though, I was frustrated. I felt like they were pushing us off to the ER; I didn't realize the work they were doing behind the scenes to expedite things, and to get Dennis what he needed.

Even with this "fast track" process, we'd still be four or five hours in the ER every time. It seems that, by the time we'd get into an exam room, wait around, explain everything to the nurse, wait some more, explain everything again to the doctor, maybe wait again for someone to take him for a CT scan, and then wait for a room to be ready upstairs, many hours would pass. Sometimes a friend or family member would accompany us; sometimes it was just me. Never the kids—ER visits were way too long for their taste, and plenty of family or friends were happy to watch them on a moment's notice.

Dennis could get hospital food if he was hungry, but I was on my own when it came to that. So, more than once, I texted a nearby friend, requesting any sort of food that wasn't from a vending machine. The first time she brought takeout to the ER, she brought pho—saying she thought the bone broth would be good for me—so that became our little tradition. Eventually, I found some food delivery app and could arrange for the delicious noodles to arrive myself.

Once Dennis was admitted, there was still more for me to do. You might think that, once he was in the hospital, I could sit back and let the medical team takeover. But, I learned that as a caregiver—the one who was with Dennis all the time, and the one who had been speaking with all of the various specialists involved in his case—I played an important role in ensuring he got the right care. I had to brief the floor nurse on his situation, including what medications he was on and when he'd last had them. Most meds he was on at home, they didn't want me to bring in; the nurses had to administer them from their supply. The exception was the chemotherapy pills. I don't know what made them so special, but those I had to bring from home. So, before every ER visit, I had to grab enough chemo pills to get by for a few days, just in case he was admitted. Then there was a whole protocol for checking in and verifying what was brought from home.

Eventually Dennis would be settled, and it was time for me to go home. Since the first two nights he was in the hospital, when I stayed with him, I'd been sleeping at home every night. As my neighbor, whose husband also died of brain cancer, said when she called me the morning of Dennis's first surgery, this was to be a marathon, not a sprint. I had two kids at home who needed me, too—so continually farming them out to others while I slept at the hospital didn't seem a viable plan.

Sometimes, after Dennis was admitted, it was after midnight before I could head home. I'd have to go back down to the ER and find a security guard to walk me to my car. More than once, I left the hospital with my car running on fumes, and not at all certain that I could make it back across the bridge without running out of gas. I was logging a lot more miles on the road than usual, and didn't always stay ahead of the keeping-gas-in-the-car game. When this happened, I'd stop at a gas station near the hospital, and quickly pump a couple gallons of gas—just enough to get home—to minimize the time I was standing out in public in not-the-safest-neighborhood at two in the morning.

At least there wasn't any traffic getting home at that time.

20

Today is a better day
June 8, 2015

Dennis is doing much better today than yesterday. I was very surprised to see him sitting in the chair watching TV today when I arrived at the hospital. At this point, the plan is for discharge tomorrow, with home visits by PT, OT, Speech, and nursing. We will all look forward to having him home again.

In other news, I arrived home from the hospital today to find our fireplace completely transformed. Stunning. New rock facing was installed. And, as we speak, installation of baseboard and casing is beginning. Thanks so much to the wonderfully angelic people making this happen.

The families at St. Louise really were incredible in their support. With the installation of the fireplace facing and baseboards, our unexpected remodel was largely complete. I still had to coordinate installation of the countertops and new refrigerator, but that required just a few scheduling phone calls. Family and friends stepped in to wait at the house for the deliveries while I was at the hospital.

I don't know what I'd do without such supportive allies.

Discharged
June 9, 2015

Quick update: Dennis has been discharged after
two nights at the hospital. Daily radiation
continuing. Home health visits will start this
week.

Today was supposed to be a good day
June 9, 2015

Dennis came home today, but his severe
headache persisted...so now we are back at ER.
Waiting for another CT scan, consult with
neuro team, and such.

This is the 4th ER visit in about a week.

———

F our trips to the ER in a week. Like I said, we had enough
medical encounters in eight months to last us a lifetime.

Surgery tomorrow
June 10, 2015

Tomorrow the neuro team is going to place a
shunt to relieve pressure in Dennis's brain.
This should hopefully relieve his headaches.
He will stay in the hospital tonight and
tomorrow night--after that TBD.

_____

Surgery postponed
June 11, 2015

Today started out with déjà vu. Exactly 4
weeks ago today, we were sitting in the same
area of the hospital waiting for Dennis to
come out of surgery. This morning the plan was
to do a procedure to place a shunt, to relieve
pressure in his brain. Dennis had been taken
to pre-op and anesthesia, and we were settling
in to wait, when the surgeon and anesthesiologist came out to say that Dennis had mentioned
that he'd just eaten a cookie. So they are
postponing surgery--perhaps until this afternoon, evening, or tomorrow morning.

Thanks everyone one for your continued support
and kind messages.

Update: Surgery will be at 7:40am tomorrow.

This first month or so of Dennis's illness, it felt like each and every day was a lifetime unto itself. I'd been back-and-forth across the I-90 bridge more times than I probably had been in the previous decade. There were so many visits to doctors, trips to the ER, and inpatient stays. So many detailed discussions of his condition, of medications, and procedures. I felt like I'd swallowed the *Cliffs Notes* version of "Med School 101."

And now, we found ourselves sitting in the same lobby of the hospital where we'd been exactly four weeks earlier, when this whole ordeal started. For all the terminology I'd learned, it turned out there was a really important term that was still foreign to me: NPO. It's some Latin abbreviation for "nothing by mouth." Basically, it means fasting. No food. No water. You're having surgery, so you've got to have an empty stomach.

Early that particular morning, I'd breezed into his room to see him before surgery, right past a big sign on the door: "NPO." It didn't mean anything to me, so I didn't even notice it. I apparently also wasn't remembering anything I'd known from my own previous wrist and knee surgeries, because when Dennis wanted to eat a delicious-looking cookie on his nightstand, I encouraged it.

I was surprised, a bit later, to see the surgeon appear in the lobby with the anesthesiologist. I wasn't expecting to see him for a few hours, when he would come to report that surgery was complete.

"Dennis said he thought he ate a cookie this morning," the doctor said. "Is that possible?"

"Oh. Yes. Wow. I didn't even think of that. Yes, he did."

And just like that, the whole surgery had to be rescheduled for the following day.

25

Surgery complete
June 12, 2015

Surgery to place a shunt in Dennis's head was completed this morning without issues. The surgeon said there was a lot of pressure on his cerebral spinal fluid due to the tumor's size and location. So, it's a good thing they did the procedure.

He is resting comfortably, and will stay at the hospital until at least tomorrow.

———

What I remember most about waiting for Dennis to come out of surgery on this day was lying down on the small couch in the hospital lobby and putting my sweatshirt over my head. Pretending to be asleep. It was glorious. I could rest and relax. Not worry about making conversation with anyone. Time to myself to just think. And rest.

It was almost as if I knew how long the road ahead would be. The shunt they put in was an attempt to relieve the pressure in Dennis's brain. They installed some sort of device on the right side of his head, toward the back, and also put in a tube that took extra cerebral spinal fluid (CSF) from his brain and diverted it to his abdomen. The buildup of fluid was creating pressure in his brain and causing headaches—sometimes severe headaches. I think the idea was that sending it to the abdominal cavity would get it out of the confined space in the brain, and cause it to be reabsorbed by the body.

After the surgery was over, I dashed back across the lake to attend last-day-of-school festivities with the kids. I was late, so I squeezed in where I could. I felt like all eyes were on me.

As usual.

Johnny Cash and Thomas Hobbs
June 13, 2015

Dennis was feeling better today. By afternoon,
he didn't seem to have much of any headache.
His awareness of the gravity of his situation
was also better. We talked. Which was good.
But very hard. Actually, it was pretty much
the worst thing ever.

I am not sure when he is coming home. Monday
we talk about next steps with social worker,
doctor, etc. Tomorrow, when Peter returns from
camping, I'm taking the kids to see him.

Tonight, after Megan was asleep, I pulled out
my guitar and practiced some songs, for the
first time in a while. My fingers are now sore
from the strings. I practiced a couple of
Johnny Cash songs--"I Walk the Line" and "Ring

of Fire"--for Dennis. I practiced The Beatles'
"Let It Be" for myself. And I practiced
"They'll Know We Are Christians By Our Love"
for so many of you.

Last week I was thinking about *Of Mice and
Men*, and high school English literature
classes. Today I'm thinking of college political science class. I remember that Thomas
Hobbs said something to the effect of "life is
solitary, poor, nasty, brutish, and short."
(Isn't that awful??) Anyway, he was wrong on
point one. Life is not solitary. Nor should it
be. You all have proved him wrong.

It's a bit odd to hear from so many people
from every chapter of our lives. But at the
same time, so wonderful. Thank you, and please
do keep reaching out as you are able. Your
messages mean so much. Some people have said
I'm handling things well. I have no idea if I
am or not, but there are two things I do know:
I am doing the best I can, and that will have
to be enough.

W hen I wrote this post, I wasn't ready to share what
actually happened that day. What I wrote was true, but
it lacked details. Here's how it went down.

"I'm walking into the hospital to tell Dennis he's dying and
needs to write cards to the kids," I texted to an old college friend,

who was also dealing with a critically ill husband. "This is the hardest fucking thing I will ever have to do."

You see, another of my wise and thoughtful friends had suggested I get Dennis to write cards to the kids. Notes they could open on future occasions, like graduations and wedding days and eighteenth birthdays. I thought that sounded like the worst idea in the world.

And, sadly, probably a good one.

It was pretty clear to me by this point that he would not likely live to see our then eight- and ten-year-olds graduate, get married, or have kids. It wasn't even clear if he would live until Christmas.

Nothing in Dennis's situation gave me hope that he would be one of the single digit statistics who survive this type of brain cancer. It seemed we were always "playing defense" — dealing with infections and cerebral spinal fluid leaks and major cognitive issues.

By now the realization was dawning on me: I needed to start preparing for the future. A future where my kids would have a dead dad.

I had no idea where to start. Asking Dennis to write cards to the kids seemed as good a place as any.

Even if it did sound dreadful.

The hardest part about embarking on a card-writing plan was that Dennis didn't remember that he was dying. He'd been in the conversations with the neurosurgeon and oncologist. He heard the results each time there was a new scan. The doctor shared with him his diagnosis.

And yet, on any given day, he didn't remember that he was terminally ill.

Glioblastoma is insidious like that. It affects people differently, depending on where in the brain it is; in his case, it affected his short-term memory. I still remembered being a fly on the wall when the speech therapist's question about the relative sizes of dogs and horses had stumped him—so I had no idea how I would broach the subject of him writing cards to the kids.

Then, one Saturday morning as I was home making pancakes, I was shocked when I picked up a call from an unknown number to find him on the other end of the line. Dialing home from the hospital phone system was confusing. Perhaps a nurse dialed for him; I'll never know.

Anyway, I don't remember any of the conversation except for one critical point: he expressed a bit of frustration at the confusion he felt. I clearly remember his conclusion: "I guess that's just the way I am now."

This was the most awareness he had exhibited in the month since his first visit to the neurosurgeon. And so, I knew that it was now-or-never if I was going to have a conversation with him about writing cards to the kids. I made arrangements for a friend to watch them, and headed back across the bridge into the city.

I swooped into a big box store on the way—the one nearest the freeway—which is how I ended up with their plain set of one hundred cards and envelopes. It was literally the only option they had for plain notecards that were suitable for men. I was in no position to run all over town looking for other options, so a package of a hundred cards it was.

I can't even begin to describe the level of dread I felt walking into that hospital on that day. It wasn't just that my husband of nearly seventeen years was terminally ill—as if that wasn't bad enough—but my angst was compounded by the fact that I would have to break the news to him, all over again, that he was dying.

At this writing, five years later, I can still conjure up the exact feeling I had that day, starting as I drove toward the hospital, climbing with each passing mile—and culminating in near revulsion as I entered the hospital lobby. That's how traumatic it was.

I texted my friend. And I decided—right then and there—that nothing else in life would really be all that terrifying if I could handle what I'd come to the hospital to do on this day.

I made my way up to Dennis's room and braced myself for the ensuing conversation. I showed him the cards and asked if he would write some notes for the kids. I didn't immediately say why. Instead, I asked if he knew what the cards were for.

"Yes," he said. "They're called 'death and dying notes.'"

"What are those?"

I wanted to know if he really understood.

"They're what you write when you only have a few months to live, and you want to write notes to the people important to you."

Yes. He does get it.

We talked. We cried. We held hands, and I thanked him for the honor of being his wife.

It was our only chance for any meaningful conversation in the whole eight months he was sick.

And, I'm happy to say that he was—barely—able to write cards to the kids. Just one card each, and he didn't even finish them. He got a couple of sentences written on each. I tried and tried to persuade him to add, "Love, Dad," but he was convinced he was going to come back and finish them later. He had more to say, but was having difficulty getting it out.

I pleaded with him to finish these first cards. He could write a second set of cards if he had more to say later. After all, we had ninety-eight more cards in the package. Alas, no such luck. He was determined to add more thoughts to these initial cards later, before signing them.

Of course, later never came. When I was back at the hospital the very next day, it was clear that he wasn't going to have the awareness necessary to finish them. I quietly removed the cards for safekeeping, and that was that.

I later lamented to my friend—the one who suggested the cards in the first place—the fact that he didn't finish them. She said, "Well, you're just going to have to explain to the kids someday that he didn't finish them, because he had more to say."

She was right, of course.

I learned something about myself that day, too:

I can do hard things.

Which, it turns out, would become an imperative down the road. Eventually I was going to have to figure out how to be a solo parent. Not only that, but a solo parent under challenging circumstances.

For now, though, it was enough to try to get us all through each day.

We were in survival mode.

27

Sunday & Monday
June 15, 2015

Sunday was a better day than Monday. The kids
and I enjoyed a nice visit with Dennis in the
afternoon. He also enjoyed visits with other
family members throughout the day. When we
were there, we played a game and did a puzzle.
(This puzzle, which was 100 pieces and age 5+,
was actually pretty hard--it was all gray
rabbit fur and pink flowers, and the piece
cuts were odd. Ugh.) Anyway, Dennis didn't
have much of any headache, and seemed to enjoy
the visits.

Today, however, he wasn't feeling well. This
afternoon he had a fever, headache, and looked
tired. By the time I left this evening, the
fever was gone, but the headache persisted.

They are running labs and checking for potential infections.

Someone mentioned that the Johnny Cash songs I
was practicing were appropriate for Dennis. I
guess that's lucky--because those are the only
Johnny Cash songs I know. :)

By the way, I'm sure you all know that there
are many family members, near and far,
grieving Dennis's illness. I know you will
remember to keep them in your thoughts and
prayers as well. This is so hard for everyone.

———

When someone is in the hospital, or a skilled nursing facility, or ill at home, there are a lot of hours to fill in any given day. When the Mariners weren't playing—or later, the Seahawks or Huskies—we sometimes tried playing games or cards to pass the time.

Sadly, Dennis's brain cancer made many games pretty difficult to play. But, since Peter and Megan were still young, we had kid board games around. Games like Sorry.

One of the most heartbreaking memories I have is Megan helping Dennis play Sorry. It was a complete role reversal, with her coaching him through playing. She was so cheerful about it. So confident. So kind.

It must have been breaking her inside.

It's only been recently that we've been able to talk about how hard that was for her. How I wish I had talked about it with her at the time. Separately, privately, later that same day. So she could "let out" how she really felt, instead of keeping it bottled up.

She did such a good job keeping a positive demeanor in front of him. I think I was relieved that she "seemed" OK, and it was one less thing I needed to worry about. I had plenty on my plate as it was.

But now, with the benefit of hindsight, I can't imagine she was really OK. I wish I had started a dialogue with both kids much sooner, letting them know it was normal to be worried. Safe to talk about their fears. OK to feel whatever they were feeling at any given moment.

I think it would have helped the future grief process tremendously.

28

Tuesdays seem to be bad days
June 16, 2015

Today they discovered the cause of Dennis's
fever: deep vein thrombosis, in both legs.
They have started anticoagulants. They did
another CT scan, and cannot determine the
cause of the continued headaches.

Today he was discharged to a skilled nursing
facility nearer our home. Unfortunately, it's
11:30 p.m. and I'm still here trying to sort
out medications. The anti-coagulant should be
arriving from the pharmacy any time ... but
has not yet.

Last Tuesday, when Dennis was discharged to
home, we ended up back at ER that same night.
Today, these developments. I hope this does
not become a pattern on Tuesdays.

Update: medication finally arrived and was
administered.

———

M aybe I had too much faith in "the system."
People warned me when Dennis first got sick
that I would need to be his advocate. I listened and made a
mental note—but deep down, I didn't know what this
meant. Why wouldn't things just "work" as they were
supposed to? I'm sure this sounds quite naïve, but at the
time, I had no experience with the medical system in any
significant way, save for the usual preventative visits, maybe
an orthopedic surgery here or there, and some trips to
urgent care.

Dennis's brain cancer initiated me into the health care world
in a big way. And, I found, I was pretty good at navigating it. I
still remember the ER visit when the doctor turned to me and
said, "Are you a medical professional of some sort?"

"No," I said, complimented that he thought I might be. "I'm
an IT person. I've just learned a lot in the past month."

When the next nurse came in, the doctor waved his hand in
my direction and said to her, "She's not a nurse, even though she
sounds like one."

You see, I had learned really well how to summarize
Dennis's situation whenever we had a new encounter with the
medical system. When we saw his usual team, this was of course
unnecessary. But often a new encounter started with an ER visit
—meaning a new doctor, and new nurses. Dennis had a chart in
the computer that I'm sure was *many* screens long. I didn't see it,
so I don't know how much was summarized at the top versus
needing to scroll through months of history to get the pertinent
facts.

I became really good at summarizing the relevant history and critical current issues.

Glioblastoma.

Original craniotomy May 14.

VP shunt put in on June 12.

Craniotomy revision on July 2.

CSF leakage and infection.

Major abdominal pain, suspected to be from the shunt diverting infected CSF to the abdomen.

IVC (inferior vena cava) filter in place for DVT (deep vein thrombosis).

On Temodar.

And on and on. The particulars varied from day to day, week to week, month to month. Any time I heard a word or acronym that was new to me, I asked what it meant—and added it to my ever-growing vocabulary. I got really good at talking their language, using the acronyms, summarizing relevant facts.

Things just seemed to work better when I did.

29

A less eventful day
June 17, 2015

Today was less eventful than recent days. So
that was good. Dennis went back to radiation
for the first time in over a week. He had
various evaluations today; sometime soon we
should be discussing therapy goals for
discharge.

Also good is that the new countertops were
installed in our kitchen yesterday. I stopped
at Home Depot this afternoon to get some
Teflon tape and a T-piece that I needed in
order to reconnect the faucet and hook up the
water line for the new refrigerator. I decided
to jog in from the parking lot because, well,
why not? I was in a hurry, and I could use
some exercise and air anyway. So I paused to
ask the greeter what aisle had plumbing parts.

He pointed me in the right direction, and I thought, well, why not jog over there, too? So I got to aisle 37 and, lucky for me, there was a Home Depot guy right there. So I pulled out the old part and told him what I needed, and he said, wait, is the water still running? It took me a moment, but then I realized that he thought I was running because the water was leaking out all over the place at home!! I assured him, no, the kitchen was fine, and the reason I was running was another whole story, which I didn't bother him with.

Anyway, tonight I re-installed the faucet and hooked up the fridge water line, so now we are one step closer to the kitchen being done :)

Tomorrow I'm not sure what to expect. The neurosurgeon wants to see Dennis again, because the original incision continues to leak, and his headaches continue.

I practiced a little more guitar tonight.

───────

Sometimes, you just want to fix your sink—and not have to talk with everyone about grief in order to do it. This trip to Home Depot would be the first time I realized that.

It's always a split-second calculation: what do I say in response to a comment out of left field that has the potential to get awkward really fast?

For example, a few years after Dennis died, I had some technicians at the house installing central air. I mentioned to one of them that I was having trouble with ants—they had just reappeared in my kitchen after being gone a while—and he offered to take a look.

His suggestion? He pulled out his phone, showed me a picture of a spray bottle, and said: "You should get some of this and have your husband spray it in the crawlspace."

Ugh. Now all of a sudden, we might end up in a death-and-dying conversation, when I'm just trying to get rid of the ants in my house. Not to mention the patriarchal shit about having my husband take care of it.

And so, I had to make an on-the-fly choice: I could say, "My husband is dead." Things would get awkward really quickly. He'd probably stumble around and not know what to say, and then I'd feel like I had to say things to help *him* feel better about the exchange. I didn't have the energy for that.

Or, I could challenge his assumption that spraying for ants was man's work. Frankly, I didn't have the energy to go there at that moment either.

I managed to let his remark fall by the wayside, neither confirming nor refuting his assumption that my husband would do it. I asked a follow-up question about the type of spray and exactly where it needed to go. And then I thanked him for the pointers on the ants, and extracted myself from the conversation.

30

I'm glad I got the faucet hooked up yesterday
June 18, 2015

It's a good thing I got the faucet in when I
had a chance. Because today & tomorrow would
probably have been out of the question.

We went back to the neurosurgeon today so he
could look at Dennis's original incision. The
one from five weeks ago. The one that should
be fully healed by now. It has been leaking...sometimes more, sometimes less. The
doctor cleaned it, swabbed it to check for
infection, and put in two stitches. But, also,
the doctor suspects that the shunt he put in
last Friday may not be working properly.

So, we will be back at Swedish in Seattle very
early tomorrow for a "shunt study"--basically
imaging with contrast dye, to determine

whether the shunt is working. If it's not,
then they will fix it tomorrow. "Fix it" means
another surgery. I guess, if it's needed, it
should be a shorter procedure than the others.
But still.

I will post again tomorrow when I have more
info.

31

I'm not even sure how to title this post
June 19, 2015

It's been an eventful day so far. Started with
getting stuck in the elevator at Swedish. Five
of us and a wheelchair in a very small old
elevator. Let's just say that didn't go too
well.

Then we went for the shunt study. It was
cancelled because of significant new swelling,
CT scan instead. It was looking like surgery
this evening was very likely. However, in the
end, they decided the shunt is actually working, and not to do surgery.

Dennis has had severe headache today.
Increased steroids should hopefully help. We
are on our way to Issaquah for radiation, then
back to rehab place in Redmond.

I'm not even sure what to title this post.
Maybe "it's only lunchtime and we've already
had a week's worth of activity this morning."

———

W hen I posted this, several people suggested in the
comments that the title should have some expletives in
it. I think that would have been appropriate. It was definitely
that sort of morning.

There's something else I remember about that day, something that still haunts me. In the bowels of the Swedish Cherry Hill campus, while we were waiting for the shunt study which was called off, Dennis turned to me and said: "I'm suffering."

Much more was communicated with his eyes than his words.

The swelling in his head—cerebral spinal fluid which had nowhere to go—was creating a lot of pressure. This pressure was causing a severe headache. A possible solution was to give him more steroids to control the swelling.

"We have to be concerned about potential diabetes if we increase his steroids too much," said the oncologist's physician's assistant.

"Why are we worried about diabetes?" I asked. "Isn't the brain cancer going to kill him before diabetes would?"

"Well, yes."

Umm—please ease his suffering then. If that means steroids, so be it.

32

Up and down
June 21, 2015

Saturday was a better day. Dennis was feeling
considerably better--not much headache--and
the kids and I enjoyed a nice visit with him.
We played a game. Everyone enjoyed it. It
seemed maybe the medication adjustments were
helping.

Saturday evening, the kids and I crashed on
the couch and watched a movie. Peter had been
canoeing with the Scouts all day, I felt like
I was coming down with something, and Megan
was exhausted.

Today we went to see Dennis for Father's Day.
We took brunch foods that a friend had
thoughtfully packed. Unfortunately, Dennis's
headache was much worse today. He was not able

to enjoy any sort of activity, so we just hung out together and watched kids' shows on TV. Thank you to everyone who posted Father's Day greetings for Dennis on Facebook. When he is feeling better, I will read them to him.

At least we had a good visit on Saturday.

33

Too tired to post lately; but, a fun evening tonight
June 25, 2015

I've been too tired to post much for a few days. Or maybe more precisely, too tired to think about what to post. Some people have asked how Dennis is doing. I hope the lack of posts hasn't caused anyone undue worry.

Some positive trends this week. Dennis's headache seems much better the past few days. He's had less pain meds. He still has a huge bump (a hematoma) on the back of his head. (Think of a soda can; imagine cutting it in half longwise, and sticking that on the back-right part of his head. That's about the size of it.) It's quite tender, and sometimes bothers him more than other times.

We had good visits with the radiation oncologist and the neuro-oncologist's office this
week. Radiation continues 5x week. Chemo
continues. Both will end around mid-July, then
the chemo will transition into some other
(less frequent) schedule.

He remains at a skilled nursing facility in
Redmond, not terribly far from our home. They
are working to transition him off of injection
blood thinners (for deep vein thrombosis),
onto pills for the same purpose, with the goal
of coming home approximately next week.
Assuming pain stays stable and we have no more
emergencies between now and then. The kids and
I enjoyed games with him when visiting today
and yesterday.

A friend has been organizing weekly Rosaries,
the first of which was at our house maybe a
month ago. Since then it's been held elsewhere, as it's just been too chaotic here, and
unclear what our schedule would be, with all
the ER visits and hospital stays. Tonight,
however, we held it here again. A group of
adults and kids gathered in the living room.
There were extra Mary prayers, too, since a
visiting Mary statue has come to stay for a
while.

Since we were on the Mary theme, I thought I'd
play The Beatles' "Let it Be" for the group.

As I told everyone, I don't do concerts, I do sing-alongs, so I passed out the song packets that I keep around. Right away someone spotted Kenny Rogers's "The Gambler." So, we started with that...jumped right from all the seriousness and reverence into a raucous and enthusiastic sing-along. It was great fun.

We covered some old family favorites: "Charlie on the MTA," "Take Me Home Country Roads," and "Thank God I'm a Country Boy." Also some children's hits, mostly requested by Megan, such as "On Top of Spaghetti." And of course, the songs I've been practicing lately: Johnny Cash's "Ring of Fire" and "I Walk the Line," "Let it Be," and "They'll Know We are Christians by Our Love." Everyone was so enthusiastic; I loved it.

I so rarely get to play and sing with anyone who is not eight (my Girl Scout troop) or eighty (with the Cub Scouts visiting the assisted living place). This was really great.

In my family there is a long tradition of my aunts and my dad playing guitar and singing. They've been doing family sing-alongs at all the extended family gatherings for as long as I can remember. From the time I was about eight years old, I thought it was just about the coolest thing ever, and I always intended to learn "someday"; two years ago, I finally decided it was time.

I always thought that, if I was ever going to
be a "real" guitar player, I'd want to learn
"The Gambler." Tonight I got to sing and play
with friends. I'm so glad I did. Thank you all
for coming and singing with me.

I t's funny sometimes how things come into your life at just
the right time.

For over thirty years, I'd been wanting to learn to play the
guitar "someday." I even tried in college. I had to take a fine arts
class, which was something I dreaded—but, it turned out they
offered guitar lessons to meet the requirement. Unfortunately, it
was *classical* guitar. I had absolutely no interest in this—I wanted
to strum and sing and play cowboy songs. John Denver and
1960s folk. *Fun* songs.

The songs I'd grown up hearing during lazy summer vaca-
tions at my grandparents' home in Connecticut. They had a
backyard swimming pool and humidity and a basement—all
things I didn't have much exposure to, growing up in the Seattle
suburbs—and they had visiting aunts who played guitar and
sang. Songs I knew all the words to, since I'd been hearing them
for as long as I could remember.

For me, the highlight of any get-together was Kenny Rogers's
"The Gambler." It was a long song. It had a catchy chorus. Capti-
vating verses. I don't know what it was—but for me, "The
Gambler" was the be-all-and-end-all. No family guitar sing-
along was complete without it. I promised myself that—
someday—I would learn guitar. And if I was ever going to be a
"real" guitar player, I'd learn "The Gambler."

The thing is, music was never my thing. I gave the clarinet a
whirl in fifth and sixth grades. I took some recorder lessons from

a neighbor lady. I could never sing—at all. Never did piano. Certainly never tried guitar—until that college class. I suffered through a whole year of lessons and then promptly abandoned the classical guitar.

Fast forward a couple of decades—about two years before Dennis got sick—to the time when I found myself at a camp-out with Megan's Girl Scout troop. "Camp-out" is a relative term; the girls were in kindergarten, and it was our first outing—and it was pouring down rain. Luckily, we had reserved a rather nice cabin at the local Girl Scout property. One of the moms who came on the trip said she played guitar, so we planned an evening "campfire" (indoors, with battery candles) and sing-along. The girls, being all of five or six years old, lost interest after a few songs. But I was captivated.

That very next Monday after the weekend trip, I dug Dennis's old guitar out of the garage. I still had my nylon string classical guitar, but that was not at all suitable for the types of songs I wanted to learn. Fortunately, Dennis had a steel string guitar from his teenage years. I don't think he ever really played much, but he said he had enjoyed messing around with it.

I Googled "guitar repair" and went into a local shop that very afternoon.

"I want to learn to play guitar," I said. "Can I use this guitar, or is it in too bad of shape?"

"It's fine," the repair guy said. "Nothing wrong with it. A new set of strings, and you'll be good to go."

I walked out with new strings and an appointment for my first guitar lesson.

The only problem with this plan was that I'd have to learn to sing first. Also, I had no interest in learning music theory, nor anything complicated, nor any songs that I didn't care about. No "Twinkle, Twinkle, Little Star." It was "The Gambler" or bust.

My first lesson I told the teacher exactly this.

"What do you think? Can we do it?"

"Absolutely," he said.

And so, the first *many* months of "guitar" lessons—for which I dutifully toted my instrument each week—actually turned out to be *singing* lessons. Which I needed—desperately. There were maybe a few guitar notes thrown in here and there, mostly so I could learn to match the note on the guitar with my voice. Eventually, we turned to simple chords and simple strum patterns.

One of the first songs I learned was "This Land Is Your Land." It has three chords and easy strumming. Plus, it had the advantage that I knew the song well. Even today, I really can only play songs I know well, so that the melody and timing are second nature. If I had to interpret those from sheet music, I'd be in trouble.

I remember the very first time I played in front of an audience. It was Veteran's Day, and the Cub Scouts were going to sing for the residents at a nearby assisted living place. We had an excellent guitar player among the Scout leaders, and he'd heard that I played. He asked if I wanted to bring my guitar along. I agreed—and told him that the only song I could do was "This Land Is Your Land." At that point, I'd only been taking "guitar" lessons for around six months, and actually most of that time was the singing lessons. I practiced that song a lot leading up to that day, but still managed to flub it. It was fun anyway.

Eventually, it was time to tackle "The Gambler." I had practiced that song in the tiny lesson room so many times, and I had no idea that the guys working in the music store could hear me through the walls. Finally, after weeks of working on the song— both the vocals and guitar part—I emerged from my lesson one day to find the guys behind the counter had turned on a little music box wind-up toy that played "The Gambler." They thought it was hilarious. I was a bit embarrassed to know they'd been hearing all my amateur attempts.

This brings me to the evening I wrote about in this journal entry. I'm pretty sure this was the first time I'd ever played for, and sung with, a group of friends. At this point, I'd only been playing for a couple of years, and my only real opportunities to play were with the Girl Scouts—some of whom did eventually come to like the John Denver songs. So this was a big deal for me, to have fifteen or twenty people in my living room, and to play and sing with them. They were kind enough to indulge me.

And, actually, I think they had a good time.

Thinking about how many years—decades, actually—I'd deferred my dream of learning to play the guitar, I find it remarkable that I finally took it up not long before Dennis got sick. It turned out to be such a meaningful part of processing this journey. I remember the nights I spent up late—with everyone in bed—practicing for myself, and pondering life. The guitar became a thoughtful—and thought-provoking—companion for me on the journey.

Along with the blogging, it was helping me find my voice.

Here's the thing about "The Gambler," and specifically the chorus: "You've got to know when to hold 'em, know when to fold 'em." It was an apt metaphor for my situation. To me, it represented an admonition not to give up. To find a way forward. It would have been so easy at that time, and later after losing my husband—and my assumed future—not to figure out how to really *live* for my remaining years. To just kind of *exist*. In Kenny Rogers' words, to "fold 'em."

And folding, I think, would take an existing tragedy, and make it doubly tragic.

As I practiced my guitar for myself, in the middle of the night, while my terminally ill husband slept downstairs and my kids upstairs, I came to the realization:

There was no way I was going to fold 'em.

34

Readmitted to Swedish
June 26, 2015

We are back at Swedish again. Dennis was readmitted today. Probably just for one night, but
we are waiting for the neuro team to come back
after reviewing the new CT scan.

I picked up Dennis this morning at the skilled
nursing facility to take him to radiation. As
he leaned over to put on his shoes, he said he
thought he was "dripping." Sure enough, the
original incision, six weeks old, was leaking
significant amounts of fluid. It seems that a
stitch that was added last week broke open
today. I'll spare you guys all the gory
details.

Long story short, we went back to the ER at
Swedish in Seattle after getting radiation at

Swedish Issaquah. They decided to admit him
again so the neuro team could evaluate him. It
seems that the most likely course of action is
for the neuro fellow to come back this
evening, add stitch(es), make a change to the
setting on the shunt, and keep him overnight
to make sure everything is OK before
discharging him back to the nursing facility
tomorrow. But, we are waiting for the doctor
to come back and confirm. It's possible that
they will decide they need to do something
else. Just don't know yet.

This is the fourth admission at Swedish Cherry
Hill in the past six weeks.

35

Long couple of days
June 27, 2015

Since my last post Friday evening, too much
has happened. The summary is that Dennis was
discharged today, then readmitted due to additional leaking from his incision. The leak, by
the way, is cerebral spinal fluid.

Last night (i.e. Friday), the doctor eventually came back (around 9:30 p.m.) and re-
stitched the open hole that was leaking. I
left, and they kept him there overnight. As of
this afternoon, he hadn't had any additional
leaking, so they decided to discharge him back
to the skilled nursing facility (SNF). He and
I left the hospital about 4:15, and he seemed
fine. Not really any headache, either. When we
got to the SNF about 5 p.m., he felt light-
headed when he got out of the car. We walked

to the entrance and he sat down so I could get
a wheelchair--and a bunch of fluid leaked out.
I called the on-call neuro doctor (same doctor
he'd seen Friday), and he said, unfortunately,
I needed to bring him back to the hospital--
meaning to the ER, since it's a weekend.

So, back to Seattle we went. We were literally
at the SNF for about five minutes before we
were back out the door. Dennis was out of the
hospital a total of about two hours, and that
was nearly all drive time. We went back to the
ER. They paged neuro when we got there, and
immediately said they'd re-admit him without a
bunch of fuss. (Though they didn't do anything
to him in the ER, we were still there several
hours waiting for admission to happen.)

Finally they got a bed--the exact same room
he'd been discharged from just hours earlier.
It still took a while to get up there, touch
base with the nurse, wait for X-ray, sort out
what to do about the chemo pills, etc. Fortunately, it was the same nurse he had last
night, who was surprised to see us back so
soon. Same transport guy who had taken us to
our car this afternoon. Same triage nurse in
ER. Same doctor. Same security guard to walk
me back to my car late at night. Same, same,
same. Too bad we weren't just still there.

It was nearing 10 p.m. by the time I left.
Next steps are not yet clear, but it seems

fairly likely that a surgery will be needed,
perhaps Monday, to fix the shunt. Of course,
the prospect of surgery is complicated by the
fact that he is on blood thinners. Once the
doctors evaluate that and the X-ray, they will
call tomorrow (Sunday), presumably with a
plan.

———

Reviewing this now, it's hard to believe it had been just six
weeks since Dennis's first surgery at this point. This
initial part of the journey was characterized by a lot of *activity*.
Activity being, of course, of the undesirable variety. Trips to the
ER. Inpatient stays. Office visits. Radiation sessions. Infections,
cerebral spinal fluid leaks, and pain. *So much activity.*

This couple-day period might have been the peak of frenzy
and uncertainty. Cerebral spinal fluid was still leaking from his
six-week-old incision. The incision that should have been healed
shut by now. The CSF issues were causing, at varying times,
pressure, headaches, infections, and of course, leaks. Sometimes
drips, sometimes much more.

Being discharged from the hospital to the skilled nursing
facility, only to have to turn around and head straight back to
the hospital—and have to go back through the ER to get readmitted, after having done the *exact* same thing the day before—
might have been the height of drama and madness. Being readmitted to the *exact same hospital room* that we'd left just hours
prior was icing on the cake.

As hard as all this activity and uncertainly was on me, I
realize now how hard it must have been on the kids. When I
look back over the events of this two-day period—many hours in
the ER, two days in a row, plus me at the hospital very late both

nights—I wonder where the kids were during those times. And this was only two days—two days that were representative of the whole eight months.

I mean, I know generally where they were—with family, or with one of the many friends helping us. They were fed, they were safe, they were occupied.

But what did they think of me being gone so long? And not knowing when I'd be back? Were they scared the whole time, and not feeling like they had anyone to talk to? When I did get home, did I just check in on how their days went and tuck them in, or did I still have energy to dive deep with them—and really listen to them?

Knowing what I know now about children and grief, as I've mentioned, I wish I'd tried harder to open conversations with the kids sooner. I never lied to them about the situation, and I told them as soon as we had the diagnosis that the doctors couldn't fix it. I gave them updates on what was happening each time we saw the doctor or visited the hospital. All of that was critically important. But, I now don't think it was enough. I don't know that I was sufficiently proactive in talking with them about *their* experiences. And listening to them.

I'd like to think I could have done a better job of this—but if I'm being honest with myself, I'm not sure I could have. I didn't have the requisite knowledge, and I didn't have the bandwidth to seek it out while I was juggling caregiving and all that it entailed. I try not to beat myself up about it now, and to know that it's not too late to have these conversations.

Now is better than never.

Quick status update
June 29, 2015

The doctors are still watching the incision
for leaking. They did not do surgery today
(Monday), nor do they plan to tomorrow.

They did do a small procedure today to place a
screen to catch any blood clots that might
potentially break free.

I hope to have more information tomorrow on
whether they think the shunt is actually
working or not.

Surgery again Thursday
July 1, 2015

Brief update: Dennis had additional leaking of
cerebral spinal fluid last night. Surgery is
planned for Thursday afternoon to try to fix
the shunt and also re-close the original incision. Today he was tired and had headaches.
Hopefully relieving the pressure in his head
will help.

Surgery complete
July 2, 2015

Surgery was completed today without complications. Dennis is awake and resting in the ICU.
Tomorrow he will probably move back to the
regular neuro floor.

The doctors decided at the start of the
surgery that the shunt does appear to be working, so they didn't touch that. They went back
into the original incision and did some repair
and closed it up tightly.

Quick status
July 5, 2015

Dennis is back on the regular neuro floor at
Swedish in Seattle, after two nights in the
ICU. They kept him there an extra night due to
a fever he'd developed. He seems to generally
be feeling better now, though still has some
headaches. We should know more about the next
steps in the next few days.

The kids spent the weekend with family and
friends at our family's beach house in Oregon.
They just got home--exhausted, but had a great
time.

Roller coaster day
July 7, 2015

Today started with the expectation that Dennis
would leave the hospital and transfer to
Swedish's inpatient acute rehab unit. (Really
just one floor above where he is.) That was
supposed to happen today, perhaps tomorrow. He
was there for about a week after his first
surgery, and did well there.

Well, after a flurry of phone calls and meetings with doctors, nurses, PAs, discharge and
intake staff, and insurance, it became almost
certain that wasn't going to happen, and
instead he'd be going back to the skilled
nursing facility in Redmond. Today. Apparently
the acute rehab unit had declined to take him,
and they couldn't justify keeping him in the
hospital any more nights.

Just when this seemed inevitable, and "all" that was left to do was ensure a smooth handoff from hospital to SNF (a task that requires much detailed discussion about medications and more), the nurse came in and said that there was a new development. A culture they had taken during his surgery last Thursday had started to grow today. Translation: an infection. Just like that, the plan changed again.

So, we waited to talk to another doctor--this time the infectious disease specialist. He says the infection is near the dura (brain covering), and has decided to start IV antibiotics for 10+ days. They are placing a PICC line so that he can be discharged tomorrow and still keep the antibiotics going. Presumably he is going to the place in Redmond, but Dennis's doctor is still trying to see if he can get him into the acute rehab at Swedish.

———

This was another of those days where we had a whole month's worth of activity in one day. What started out as a relatively straightforward plan—for Dennis to transfer from the inpatient floor to the rehab floor—all fell apart by mid-day.

Initially, the problem was that the acute rehab unit declined to take him. I felt betrayed—*why wouldn't they take him?* He had just been there a few weeks earlier, and things had gone smoothly. I liked the doctor there, too.

The fact that the unit was well-integrated with the care he

was already receiving made it ideal. The neurosurgeon, neuro-oncologist, and neuro inpatient unit were all right there on the same campus. His chart was in their system. Medication hand-offs were seamless. Their unit was well-equipped with the thera-pists and facilities needed for both physical and occupational therapy. Staying there made all the sense in the world—to me.

It turns out I don't get to decide these things. I'm not clear exactly why they declined to take him, but it had something to do with his identified therapy goals not being an appropriate fit for criteria of who they would admit. Whatever. All I knew was that staying there meant a good hand off in care, and being discharged back to the skilled nursing facility meant it was pretty much on me to ensure the hand off was satisfactory. And I remembered all too well that the first hand off had been a nightmare.

When I finally resigned myself to the situation, this newly-discovered infection threw the whole plan into question again. As it turned out, infections would become a problem for much of the rest of his illness.

Dennis's birthday is coming up
July 10, 2015

Dennis did transfer on Wednesday to the
skilled nursing facility in Redmond where he
had previously been staying. He will be there
at least as long as he is getting IV antibiotics for the infection they found this week--
meaning, probably for a couple of weeks.

Dennis's birthday is coming up on July 19. He
will be 44. If anyone would like to send a
birthday card, our mailing address is:
xxxxxxxxxxxxxxxxxxxxx.

I'd love to be able to share a pile of cards
with him on his birthday. He would be so
surprised, and pleased, I think.

Dennis maybe coming home Friday...and, still time to send birthday cards!
July 15, 2015

Tomorrow we see the infection specialist. If he says no more IV antibiotics are needed, then it's likely Dennis can come home Friday! He really wants to come home. Plus, our (17th!) anniversary is Saturday, and his 44th birthday is Sunday. So, good timing. :)

Speaking of his birthday, there is still time to send a card! If you are not sure what to say, don't worry, nothing profound is necessary. A simple birthday greeting works just fine. :)

Dennis has been relatively stable lately, and not much pain, though he does remain confused about many things. The tumor is just pressing on so much of his brain.

———

A lot of people were following our journey on CaringBridge. More than once, someone commented that, by sharing our experience so openly, I was helping show other people how to face a situation like terminal illness.

I felt a sort of "responsibility" to the people following our journey. Maybe it was because Sheryl Sandberg was publicly sharing her journey, so it made sense to me to do likewise. Or maybe it's just because I liked these people, and appreciated their support.

At any rate, I remember sensing that I needed to reassure people that they needn't shy away from sending a card just because they didn't know what to write. There wasn't really anything good to write, anyway. *Get well soon? Looking forward to having you back at work?* Yeah, those weren't really going to work.

I think mostly I knew that if the tables were turned, I'd want to send a card, and then I'd get stuck not knowing what to say. And probably end up not sending it. I didn't want uncertainty to stop anyone from sending a card who wanted to send one.

Fortunately, it didn't. Dennis got so many cards. I'd only suggested birthday cards for him—not anniversary cards for us —but quite a few people noticed that our seventeenth wedding anniversary was the day before his forty-fourth birthday, and sent two cards. Which was so kind.

Have I said yet that we were so lucky to be surrounded by so many amazing people, both near and far?

43

Coming home Friday
July 16, 2015

Brief update: we saw the infection specialist today. He says Dennis can stop the IV antibiotics on Friday and come home Friday afternoon.

Lots to do to get ready. Friends came for Rosary and sing-along tonight, and then a couple of friends helped me work on organizing the new kitchen. My sister is arriving in town tonight; in the morning we will work to get the rest of the house ready, get all the home medications, etc., then work with the SNF on setting up the home health visits, and then bring him home in the afternoon.

Also, last night late I finished his birthday

present: a quilt made from his old shirts.
Kids are at scout camp; Megan returns Friday
and Peter returns Saturday. Dennis was pretty
tired going to the doctor in Seattle today,
but we managed OK.

Home! (brief update)
July 18, 2015

Quick update: Dennis came home Friday afternoon. So far so good. He is happy to be home.
Megan came home from camp yesterday. Peter
will be surprised Dennis is home. I'm picking
him up from the camp bus at noon.

Quick update
July 19, 2015

Successful weekend celebrating our anniversary
and Dennis's birthday. He had enough energy
for both dinner out on Saturday, and a family
party with all the extended family at home
tonight. I will write more tomorrow after we
see doctors in the morning. Thanks for all the
cards and greetings!

One thing after another
July 22, 2015

Just when I'm thinking maybe Dennis's situation will stabilize, something else happens. It appears he has C. Diff, a nasty gut bacteria infection that can especially be acquired when one is on antibiotics and also when one is staying in a hospital or care facility. Of course, all of the above apply in his case. We are waiting for lab results, but the doctor strongly suspects it based on symptoms. Since he came home last Friday, he's had on-and-off low grade fever, abdominal pain, and other issues. Assuming it's C. Diff., then they should be able to fix it with another antibiotic. Also, Friday we need to follow up with the surgeon so he can evaluate some ventricle enlargement on the most recent CT scan.

So, the projected activity count for this week is: five doctor visits, four radiation treatments, two different sets of lab work, a CT, an MRI, and an abdominal X-ray. And a zillion pills. And daily injections at home (i.e. given by me). At least that is what I expect based on what is currently scheduled through Friday--hopefully nothing gets added to that list.

Fortunately his head is feeling OK this week-- not much in the way of significant headaches. The abdominal pain is bothering him a lot, however.

Here is a recap on the weekend:

Saturday: We got out to Firenze, a wonderful small Italian place near here, for our anniversary dinner. We only stayed about 45 minutes--enough to eat main courses and run. Donnie was tired. It was great that we got out, though. We came home and watched about half of the movie "Walk the Line," which is about Johnny Cash. Hopefully we can watch the rest soon.

Sunday: We had a family birthday dinner/party for Dennis in the evening. It was about 25 people, including all the kids. Everyone brought something for dinner. We grilled a flank steak, at Dennis's request. We had pies and cupcakes. Gifts. A picture of the quilt is in the "photos" section of the CaringBridge site. Three folks came over and helped with cutting and a little of the sewing, ensuring it would be done on time. :) Guitar singing around the "campfire" (we didn't actually light it because it was sooo hot). It was a nice evening. He had a good time. And was tired by the end.

Over the past few days, we have read half or so of the many birthday cards that arrived. Wow. Thank you all so much. It's been fun to read cards and messages from so many people from our current and past lives. Thanks everyone for making such an effort.

A couple of friends from Dennis's office visited tonight, and brought a very generous gift for the kids: a gift card for the Family Fun Center in Tukwila. Peter is excited about the video arcade. Megan about some jumpy thing they have. As for me, I'm hoping for the Go Kart racing and Skee-Ball. :) Hopefully Dennis can join us for part of the time.

On Dennis's birthday, this site crossed the 10,000-visitor mark. Again, wow. Thank you all so much for your support and caring.

47

Almost forgot--Tuesday's fun outing
July 22, 2015

I forgot to recount Tuesday evening's fun
outing in my earlier post!

The Ivy Center had given us four tickets to
the Seattle Storm (our WNBA team) game against
the New York Liberty last night.

My parents, sisters, and their families, were
able to get additional tickets next to ours,
so we all went. By some stroke of luck, all of
the kids had been invited to participate in a
pre-game thing. I wasn't even sure what it
was, having heard third-hand that we should go
to section 118 at 6:30 for something regarding
seeing the players. Long story short, only one
car got there in time, and it happened that
Megan and Peter got to participate in an on-

court "ball exchange" just prior to the game.
When they announce the Storm starters, they
have a kid go out and the player gives them an
autographed ball. So, both kids got mini WNBA
balls. All the kids enjoyed bouncing them
around, passing them, etc., after the game.
Megan, in particular, was so excited every
time "her" player scored. It was a close game,
and we lost in the end, but exciting nonetheless.

Dennis enjoyed dinner and a visit with his mom
and stepdad while we were at the game.

48

Update
July 24, 2015

Quick update: it's still not clear what is
causing Dennis's abdominal pain. The labs for
C. Diff came back negative. Neither the infectious disease doctor, nor the neurosurgeon,
think the shunt is causing the issue. (The
shunt has an internal tube that drains fluid
from the brain to the abdomen.) An abdominal
CT with contrast dye done today showed no
apparent reason for the issues.

So, the doctor wants to try an antibiotic for
a few days, and check in on Monday to see if
it's making any difference. He seems to think
it's some type of colitis / gut issue. Also,
he says that, very rarely, the C. Diff test
can come back as a false negative. So, we'll
have to wait and see if these meds help.

All this meant that we were at Swedish (two
different locations) nearly all day today,
trying to sort this out.

———

R eading this now, I wonder, again: where were the kids if I
     was with doctors and at hospitals all day long, sorting
out what was happening with Dennis's infection? I mean, I
know they were safe and cared for. But I'm struck now with the
sense that I could have done so much more, throughout
Dennis's illness, to better position them for his eventual passing.
Yes, I was juggling a lot.

I wish I could have managed just a bit more.

49

More doctor visits this week and they can't figure out what's causing pain
July 29, 2015

A quick update: they still can't figure out
what's causing Dennis's abdominal pain.
Tomorrow we go back to the doctor for that
again. For now they are trying a stronger,
supposedly more effective, C. Diff medication,
in hopes that it helps. In the meantime, he
still has fever off-and-on, and getting around
or getting into or out of a chair or bed is
difficult. This week's MRI showed some new
areas of tumor growth, and also some areas
receding.

On a brighter note, we all went to City Hall
today for lunch with Dennis's colleagues. He
enjoyed that very much.

Kids have been swimming and boating in Lake
Sammamish several times this week--a highlight
for them :)

———

Dennis's colleagues at the City of Redmond were so incredibly supportive throughout his illness. They sent many cards from the office, signed by the team. Perhaps it was weekly—it's hard to say. Individuals and small groups came over to visit him, often bringing food or gifts. On one of those visits they brought him a University of Washington Huskies baseball hat. He wore that hat all the time—and now it's one of Megan's treasured possessions.

Certainly, the most significant thing they did was to contribute hours and days from their own leave accounts to his. I'll never know who donated, or how much any individual gave, but the overall impact was that he was able to receive his full salary the entire time he was sick. Otherwise he would have had to go on disability—at a reduced rate of pay—after his own leave was exhausted. I will forever be grateful for their kindness.

This visit into City Hall for lunch with the team came at a time when his condition was poor. He was in a lot of pain from the infection. As I drove with him around that time, every little bump made him uncomfortable. Especially speed bumps—those I had to take at around five miles per hour, and even that small jostling caused him pain.

Getting Dennis up from the bed was nearly impossible. The core muscles required to sit up from a lying down position—or vice-versa, to lie down once he was sitting on the edge—were impossible for him to engage without significant pain. This left me with the physically demanding task of using my muscles in place of his, to pull his six-foot frame into a sitting position, for example. At this point in the journey, I was tired, too. Pretty quickly I realized this wasn't going to work much longer than a day or so—I would wear myself out and be unable to care for anyone.

I put in a call to the nurse case manager at his health insurance company and said I couldn't do this any longer. I told her they needed to send over a hospital bed that raised and lowered so he could get into and out of bed.

And they agreed.

Wow. I learned from that episode that I could ask for what I needed. And, that I *had* to ask. They weren't going to magically drop a hospital bed on me. It was on me to make a reasonable case for what I needed, and defend it. Now, clearly, insurance companies don't always give you want you need, even if you do make a good case. But, I learned that if I didn't ask, the answer would always be no.

50

At the ER again
July 30, 2015

We saw the infectious disease doctor again
this afternoon, and related to him Dennis's
continued pain, fever, etc. He wanted me to
take him back to ER and get him readmitted, so
they can run more tests, watch him, and hopefully figure out what is going on. He wasn't
comfortable sending him home in his current
condition. I agreed. He's exhausted, confused,
and in pain.

ER is busy today, so I guess we will be here a
while waiting for a bed. When we got here they
said the hospital was so full they were doing
"treat and transfer"--i.e. sending patients to
other hospitals after working them up here.
That would be bad, given Dennis's situation. I

called his oncologist and they are working to make sure he can stay here.

———

I'd never even heard of "treat and transfer" before this particular ER visit. The very thought of this was horrifying. I can't imagine if he'd been sent to Harborview or the UW Medical Center or one of the other local hospitals. All are top-notch hospitals, and if he didn't have terminal brain cancer, it would have been OK (if a bit of a hassle) to have him transferred to one of them.

But, he had a very long chart at Swedish. Multiple surgeries, lots of medications, many complications. His neurosurgeon and oncologist were there. Transferring to a different hospital system was, in my mind, out of the question.

Fortunately, I'd learned by then that I had to call over to the Ivy Center and get them on the case. They worked some magic behind the scenes, and eventually, he was admitted to the neuro floor at Swedish.

Which, by this point, was becoming a very familiar place.

51

A bunch of "maybes"
August 1, 2015

Dennis is still at Swedish, where the doctors
are still investigating what is going on.
Right now all we have are a bunch of "maybes"-
-it seems that maybe meningitis and peri-
tonitis are causing his issues, but that is
unconfirmed. They have started IV antibiotics
as if those were the issues while they wait
for confirmation. They drew out some cerebral
spinal fluid last night, and are waiting for
bacteria to grow in the lab. It seems we will
know more over the next few days.

Kids are enjoying a getaway at the beach house
in Oregon. I'm trying to get some things done
in between hospital visits.

I knew Dennis was in a lot of pain with this infection. I could see it on his face, and I could tell how much he hurt when attempting simple movements like going from lying down to sitting up, or from sitting to standing.

Still, I don't think I truly appreciated how much pain he was in until I myself contracted meningitis a year or so after he died.

I'd been at a women's surfing camp in Mexico, chosen because they promised to "make girls out of women." It seemed just what I needed after the hell I'd been through. The experience was everything I hoped for, and more—but, upon my return, I developed incredible pain in my back and neck. At first, the doctors thought I'd "overdone it." After all, a week of surfing was quite a bit more strenuous than my usual sit-at-a-desk-all-day routine. Eventually they discovered that it was not muscular-skeletal pain—it was viral meningitis.

I was so sick that it took me *days* to even have the energy to watch Netflix in my bed. Dennis's meningitis was bacterial rather than viral. Which was apparently worse.

He was a real trooper.

52

Quick update--shunt infection
August 4, 2015

A brief update: the doctors have decided that
Dennis has an infection in/around the shunt
that they placed in his head in June. The
cerebral spinal fluid is also infected, making
it a form of meningitis. It's apparently the
same type of bacteria as the original infection of the brain covering about a month ago.
There was talk of removing the shunt, but they
have decided not to do that until/unless he
develops more complications.

Basically, they are going to place a new PICC
line and begin a few weeks of antibiotics. He
has been receiving some broad-spectrum antibiotics while they waited to see what was going
on, and does seem to be much improved from how
he was late last week. Much less pain, less

fever. Confusion remains significant, however. It's unclear at this time how long he will be in the hospital. It was another long day at the hospital, waiting for information and for plans to develop.

———

"Confusion remains significant."

I can't be sure, but this may have been the time he didn't recognize me.

I didn't tell anyone about it at the time, and didn't blog about it. I'm not sure why. I guess a few experiences during this journey were just for me.

Discharged today; home now
August 7, 2015

Dennis was discharged today, and is now home.
He is tired, but feeling much better than a
week ago.

He will have another week or so of IV antibiotics. Home Infusion Services trained me today
in how to handle the IV--hooking up new bags
and lines, flushing the line, using the
pump, etc.

We also had a hospital bed and wheelchair
delivered today. There were some logistical
frustrations with the medical equipment
company, but we got through them. He is able
to walk around the house, but needs the wheelchair for appointments as it's tiring for him
to walk very far.

Peter leaves for a week-long fifty-mile canoe campout with his Scout troop tomorrow. On the trip, he will be responsible for three meals and a dessert for twelve people, and two additional meals for four people. He has been practicing his meals at home, and is ready to go. Megan will be doing a choir day camp at St. James Cathedral next week.

———

By now, we were nearly three months into Dennis's illness. He had been in so much pain in recent weeks, and so tired and generally struggling, that I was quite worried about Peter's weeklong canoe trip.

Peter had been training with the Scouts all summer and was slated to go away—totally off-the-grid—for a seven-day trip, paddling the length of Ross Lake, in North Cascades National Park. He had responsibility for planning and cooking certain meals for the group, plus he had to hold up his end of paddling a two-man canoe for fifty miles. At age ten—nearly eleven—he was to be the youngest Scout on this trip.

I wasn't worried about Peter. I was worried that Dennis would die while he was gone. And that I wouldn't be able to reach Peter, nor get him back home if need be.

I had a long discussion with the trip leader, and in the end, decided to take a gamble and send Peter on the trip. It eased my mind a bit that one of the adults arranged to rent a satellite phone in case of emergencies (of any type).

I'm glad he went. The trip was—and still is—a highlight of his young life so far.

Quick update
August 14, 2015

Quick update: we saw infection doctor today.
IV antibiotics will continue at home for
another week, then switch to high dose oral
antibiotics for a long time (perhaps perma-
nently). It's a continuous drip, so he has a
small bag with a pump in it that is attached
to his right arm via a PICC line. Every 12
hours I change the bag, tubes, flush the PICC,
reset the pump, etc. I am getting quite
skilled at managing all that. :)

Monday will be the last radiation session.
Maybe he will be less tired once that is done.

A h, radiation. Dennis was supposed to have thirty sessions of radiation—five days per week, for six weeks.

He did get thirty sessions, but it took nearly twice that long to fit them all in. Every time he was back in the hospital, radiation had to be cancelled. And he was in the hospital a lot in these early months.

This was partly a logistical issue (he was receiving radiation at a different Swedish campus, nearer our home), and partly, as I recall, an issue of something interfering with something else. Maybe radiation interfering with some medication, or vice versa. I can't remember what. It doesn't really matter, anyway.

Apparently, there is a tradition in cancer clinics to have patients ring a bell when they complete their course of radiation or chemotherapy. It's supposed to signal the end of active treatment, and the beginning of a life free of cancer. It's supposed to be celebratory.

When Dennis's last day of radiation finally came, they congratulated him. And had him ring the bell. We took pictures. It was perfunctory, and I knew it.

I wish we'd skipped it.

New chapter begins next week; and, kicking the elephant out of the room
August 27, 2015

Everyone is in bed, and I'm here thinking about next week. Next week begins a new chapter: the kids return to school, and I return to work. Oh boy.

There has been a lot of activity on this site for the past few months. That is because there has been a lot of activity in Dennis's situation. ("Activity" is not a good thing in this case.) So first, a quick summary of the situation to date:

Dennis was diagnosed with glioblastoma in May. I started noticing symptoms on May 1--odd and subtle memory loss and confusion that got markedly worse over a week or so. By mid-May

he was having his first surgery. The intent
had been to remove as much of the tumor as
possible, but as it turned out, they could
only safely get enough for a biopsy, and could
not do any tumor removal.

At our first meeting with the neuro-oncologist, we learned that Dennis has a grade 4
glioblastoma--an aggressive brain cancer that
can't be fixed--as well as a lower-grade
glioma. All in all, that means lots of cancer
cells spread all around throughout the fabric
of his brain. Not what you hope for when you
hear "tumor"--not a discrete lump that can be
removed.

Since Dennis's first surgery on May 14, he
has been an inpatient in the hospital
numerous times. In fact, he's been either at
Swedish in Seattle, or at a skilled nursing
facility in Redmond, far more than he has
been home. He is currently home (for almost
three weeks now)--the most he's been home
since this started.

He's had three surgeries, two ICU stays, many
stays on the neuro floor of the hospital, two
stays at the nursing facility, and maybe seven
or eight ER visits, most of which have
resulted in admissions. Twice now he's been
discharged, only to be re-admitted via ER the
exact same day. He's had many complications--
deep vein thrombosis, cerebral spinal fluid

(CSF) infection, major CSF leaking, and
concussion, to name a few.

He has finally finished his course of radiation and chemo. (All the complications and
unplanned surgeries resulted in many cancelled
radiation sessions.) Our next visit with the
neuro-oncologist will be mid-September, with a
new MRI at that point to give a better idea of
the updated situation. The last MRI, maybe a
month ago, showed some areas where the tumor
had receded with the radiation, as well as
some areas of new tumor growth.

So, for now, Dennis is home. It is good, though
not easy. He has a lot of medications, which are
manageable. He can get around the house, though
we have a wheelchair, walker, and gait belt to
provide varying levels of assistance and safety
for moving about outside the house. Those
things are all manageable. Most difficult is
the fact that he has severe short-term memory
loss and confusion. This means a few things:

- An adult has to be here 24/7

- He is generally confused about what time of
day it is, e.g. waking up from a nap in the
afternoon, thinking it's the next day, and
wanting to shower and dress for the new day.

- He often thinks we live in either New York,

Portland, or Missouri (varies each day). He often doesn't recognize our house as our home, thinking instead that we are visiting, and asking when we are going home.

- Using the stove, sharp knives, etc., is out of the question, as is driving.

- He generally doesn't remember what he did earlier in the day, or even an hour before.

- He tends to fill in the gaps with incorrect memories or ideas, such as wondering where our "other" (non-existent) pets are, or telling the speech therapist that he recently took up lacrosse (not true).

And, for better or for worse, he doesn't really remember why he is so sick, nor does he remember how grave his situation is.

On the positive side, his long-term memory is good, and he remembers family and friends. He likes to watch Mariners and Seahawks games on TV, as well as Food Network and CNN. He enjoys visitors.

I am summarizing Dennis's situation in some detail, because I know some things will be awkward as we begin our new chapter next week. We will see people at school that we haven't seen all summer. I will be returning to work,

and interacting with many people for the first
time in a while.

Side note: my managers at IBM have been
incredibly kind and compassionate in how
they've handled our situation, and have given
me plenty of time and space that has been much
appreciated.

I know this will be awkward--probably more for
everyone else than for us. After all, we are
living this every day. There is a huge "elephant in the room," and I am pretty sure that
people may wonder whether to say something,
what to say, whether they will upset me by
saying something, etc. Please don't worry.
Generally speaking, saying something is better
than saying nothing--it gets the elephant out
of the room. You can always say something
simple ("I'm so sorry you're going through
this" comes to mind). Profundity not required.

I would be remiss if I didn't once again thank
the many people--family, friends, acquaintances, friends-of-friends, etc.--who have
been so tremendously helpful the past few
months. To everyone who has helped with the
kids, with Dennis, with meals, with the house,
the pets, and so much more: many, many thanks.
When people ask how I'm doing, I think the
most accurate answer is "still standing"--and
surely I would not be standing without the
kindness and generosity of so many.

Finally, Dennis does enjoy visitors, so please message me if you'd like to come by some time.

PS The bed alarm on the hospital bed just went off for the third time during the course of composing this post. I sure hope we get some sleep tonight.

———

S*till standing.* I think this is a pretty good description of where I was at this point.

I felt like I needed to write this comprehensive summary of the situation for people who were following along, in anticipation of the kids' return to school, and my return to work, the following week. I knew that we'd be seeing many people who cared about us, and many people who would ask the dreaded question, "How *are* you?"

I also knew that it would be impossible to know who had been following every single blog post in great detail, who had seen some entries here and there, and who really didn't know what was happening besides "her husband has cancer." And I knew that trying to sort this out on-the-fly—in response to the inevitable "how are you?"—would exhaust me.

I also wanted to address the "I-don't-know-what-to-say-so-I-won't-say-anything" phenomenon. I knew that people would be afraid to say the wrong thing. Mostly, I had in mind Sheryl Sandberg's post from a couple of months before, and knew there would be a *gigantic* elephant in the room. It seemed like the right course of action to try to get that elephant out.

Thus, my detailed summary of the situation to date.

I would be remiss if I didn't add that I had come a long way as a caregiver by this point, too. Earlier in Dennis's illness, I used to be really frustrated when he said things that didn't make sense. For example, he might say, "Where's the dog?"

"Daisy? She's right there," I'd respond.

"No. The other dog."

"What other dog? There is no other dog."

"The other dog. Not this one. The other one."

And around and around like that, in circles, until I would go into the other room and scream silently to myself. And then come back for more discussion of the non-existent-other-dog. I thought that, somehow, I needed to get him to understand the correct information about how many dogs we did or didn't have.

Eventually I came to realize that some of these cognitive issues he was having were very much like you might experience with a dementia patient. And, I realized that I was only frustrating both of us by trying to convince him that there wasn't another dog. In hindsight, I think he was probably asking about our previous dog, who had died six years earlier.

When I eventually accepted that the brain cancer wouldn't let me convince him that there wasn't another dog somewhere, I became much less frustrated by these types of conversations. I realized it was much kinder—and less frustrating for both of us —to just steer the conversation off the topic. For example:

"Where's the dog?"

"Daisy? She's right there."

"No. The other dog."

"Oh." *Pause.* "Hey Daisy, let's go see Dad. Here, do you want to hold her?"

That seemed to satisfy him. And not frustrate me.

And that was, to me, a win.

56

Infection remains
September 7, 2015

So on Saturday evening we were sitting and watching Seinfeld reruns when all of sudden caller ID popped up on the TV saying "Charles Cobbs." What?? Why was the neurosurgeon calling? Well, he was calling to say that the latest lab work showed that the infection is still present. It seems the period of relative calm we've had might be coming to a close soon.

On Friday, we had a scheduled follow up with the infection specialist. He was satisfied with Dennis's status, and said to continue the oral antibiotics and return in five weeks. After we saw him, we went to see Dr Cobbs. I'd called his office that morning to report that headaches had returned, cerebral spinal fluid

(CSF) was puffing out from the original craniotomy site (not leaking, fortunately, because
the incision is tight, but clearly there is
excess CSF with nowhere to go, and it's
swelling into a large bump), and confusion is
severe. They said to bring him in, and ordered
another CT. Amazingly, the CT looked fine--
fairly normal, actually. The doctor pulled a
sample of CSF, just in case, and sent us home
saying that things looked OK. We have an MRI
and big follow-up with neuro-oncology scheduled for next week, anyway, and that will
reveal more about what is going on with the
tumor, which is really the next step.

So anyway, he called Saturday to say that
preliminary lab results were back, and there
is bacteria in the CSF sample. What they don't
know yet, because they need to wait for the
bacteria to grow some more days in the lab, is
how bad it is, and also whether or not it's
the same strains as before. Basically the
question is whether the infection wasn't
really knocked out with three weeks of IV
followed by high-dose oral antibiotics, or
whether he's picked up a new infection.

So, we wait for more info. Depending on what
they find, they may re-admit him to start more
IV antibiotics, or they may need to take the
more drastic step of removing the shunt,
keeping him in ICU while the infection clears,
and then doing another surgery to replace the

shunt. For now, since he has no fever, the doctor said he can be home.

Yesterday we went to Redhook Brewery for a nice lunch with his mom and stepdad. Everyone enjoyed that. I think it's a good thing we had a nice excursion while we had the chance.

Kids are away at my parents' beach house in Oregon this weekend. They seem to be having a good time.

Funny mix of technology there this weekend--they will Facetime to say hi, and to report that they are playing 1980s Super Mario Brothers on the NES. Peter got the NES for his birthday last week--a real, vintage one. Of course I played Super Mario a lot as a kid, but havon't played it in decades, and Peter is already beating me at it easily. He actually called me a "newbie" at it. Ha! I reminded him I was playing it long before he was born.

And anyway, can you use a word like "newbie" in relation to a 1980s game, when the word didn't even exist at the time?? :)

Kids started back to school this week. So far so good there. I am re-acclimating to work. Managers and colleagues were very kind in welcoming me back. I think I'd better go try to get a few things done here before the kids get home later today.

B y now we were nearly four months into this journey, and we'd had a period of relative calm for approximately the last month. This was a significant departure from the first few months, when it seemed like every time we turned around we were either headed to the ER, or Dennis was staying in the hospital.

Infection, however, was still an issue. It seemed like we never could really get a handle on that. He had IV antibiotics in the hospital; he had IV antibiotics at home; he had high-dose oral antibiotics at various points, too. His cerebral spinal fluid was infected, so that created problems in his brain, plus the shunt that was diverting extra fluid from his brain to his abdominal cavity was sending infected fluid there, too. It was just a lot of infection for one body to fight.

It was quite the shock when the neurosurgeon called us at home on a Saturday evening. At that point he only had prelimi-nary information—that the infection was still present. He didn't yet know how bad it was, nor did he know whether this was a new infection, or whether the old one had not been eliminated with all those prior antibiotics.

We'd have to wait for the bacteria to grow a few more days in the lab before we'd get any additional information. With the partial information we did have, it seemed like the period of relative calm we'd experienced lately was about to come to an end—we just didn't know yet what that might look like.

57

Memory / Memories
September 8, 2015

Tonight, as I cooked "Pioneer Pizza" (pizza
made in a cast iron skillet), I listened to a
recording of my aunts and dad singing and
playing (on guitar) a number of old family
favorites. It was a little slice of quasi-
normalcy, at a time when normalcy is elusive,
and highly prized.

As I sang "Charlie on the MTA" along with
them, I vividly recalled singing the same song
this summer, in my living room, with a good
dozen+ people who had come to say the Rosary
and stayed to sing together. It was such a
great memory. It got me thinking about all the
other good memories I have of this summer.
(Don't get me wrong, I have plenty of other
memories that are downright awful.)

I remember each person who has dropped off food, and stayed to chat and connect.

I remember teaching Peter to sauté zucchini from the garden when he was practicing for his cooking merit badge.

I remember picking up the kids from the lake, and them begging to stay longer, to not get out of the water just yet.

I remember the happiness of receiving cards and messages from people.

I remember the late-night chats with friends who stopped by after everyone was in bed.

Speaking of everyone being in bed, I remember messing around on guitar into the wee hours of the morning.

I remember Megan getting confident with using the stove, and practicing her techniques for pancakes and assorted types of eggs.

I remember so many positives in the midst of the most awful summer ever.

I also remember some very difficult times:

The look on Peter's face, when the kids and I first discussed how the doctors can't fix Dad's cancer. Peter heard me sniffling, and

turned around in shock/surprise when he realized I was crying.

The initial meeting with his primary care
doctor, when he first said, "There's something
very wrong with your brain," and I sat there
in disbelief, saying, "Are we really having
this conversation?"

Each and every ER visit.

The time he was discharged from hospital to
skilled nursing facility, and the handoff was
handled terribly, and the needed medications
didn't arrive until after midnight, and then
only after I pushed and pushed them to fix the
problem.

I could go on, but you get the idea.

All these memories got me re-thinking about
something I've been marveling at lately: I
think it's a wonder that any of our brains
work at all. I mean, as I watch Dennis's
memory decline, I am amazed at all the things
any of us remember. Consider some basic cate-
gories of things:

Vocabulary words: Think of all the thousands
of words you know, including spelling, defini-
tion, how to use them properly, etc. And some
people know hundreds or thousands more in
another language, too. (Why do I still

remember "aus, bei, mit, nach, von, zu,
ausser, seit" from German grammar class in
high school??)

Hobbies: Think of a hobby--say, home improvement in my case--and think of all the tools,
their names, how to use them, which projects
you used them on, which saw is better for
which type of cut, for example, and on and on.

Songs: Think of all the thousands of song
lyrics and melodies you know. And commercial
jingles from decades past that are still
rattling around somewhere in your head.

Professional knowledge: A whole, vast area
that I won't even try to describe--but think
of all the details, big and small, that one
needs to know related to their job, and how
you constantly have to integrate all that into
relevant and coherent thinking related to
whatever issue is at hand.

Random memories: The name of your camp counselor when you were twelve; what happens in
all the Brady Bunch episodes; the list of
Presidents that you memorized in third grade;
and on and on and on....

How ever do we remember all these things?
Really? And how much has to get messed up--by
cancer, brain damage, etc.--in order for us to
not remember them?

When I think about how Dennis has declined so
rapidly, from someone who was working and
living life normally four months ago, to
someone who is now much like a dementia
patient, I wonder why and how any of our
brains can remember all the things I described
above, and so much more. It's really amazing
to me. If anyone here can explain how memory
works, please do.

All evening the song "Memories" from *Cats* has
been stuck in my head. Problem is, my memory
is a bit fuzzy on it (ironic, I guess :). So,
the soundtrack circling through my head goes
something like this: "Memmmmreeees, da da da
da da da daaaa / da da da da da da daaaaa / da
da da da da daaaaaa" Not too good! Maybe I'll
look it up on YouTube so I can get that
endless loop out of my head.

Now, tonight, I have no news on the infection.
I thought they might be calling as soon as
today, but they've not. I feel like the other
shoe is about to drop. He's been home about a
month; I am predicting he will be back at the
hospital soon, but I really don't know for how
long, nor whether it will be a quick in-and-
out or something longer involving another
surgery. I'll keep you all posted.

I *remember* this post well. Pun intended. Ha, ha.

Know what else I remember? Something that I most definitely did *not* write about on CaringBridge. To do so would have left me feeling *way* too exposed.

In the last chapter, I mentioned watching *Seinfeld* reruns. Since we had a lot of time to kill—and a DVD box set with all the seasons—we would from time to time watch *Seinfeld* when the kids were away. It was a nice throwback to our early-married days in New York, when we'd gather with friends to watch the Thursday night lineup.

If you've ever watched the show, I'm sure you've noticed that there a lot of sex jokes in the dialogue. At the conclusion of one such episode, Dennis turned to me and said, "Maybe we can try that sometime."

"Try what?" I asked.

"S-e-x."

He said it just like that. Spelled it out. *S-e-x*. Which, as you might imagine, was not exactly his typical way of broaching the subject.

I took a deep breath. Sex was the very *last* thing on my mind at that time. By then I was many months into being Dennis's full-time caregiver, and he had very little awareness of what was happening. It's not like we were connecting emotionally in any significant way. That time I walked into the hospital to ask him to write cards to the kids, back in June, was the one and only time we'd managed to have a meaningful discussion. By now, our relationship pretty much consisted of hanging out, watching TV together, and me organizing all his medical care.

So, I instinctively recoiled at his suggestion of *s-e-x*.

The topic itself was not exactly new. Dennis had periodically brought it up during the prior months. Each time, I'd hesitated. I mean, he had cerebral spinal fluid *leaking out of his skull*. Could physical exertion cause his head to explode? Could the chemo pills, or other medication he was taking, harm me? I didn't have any idea.

I had, by then, summoned the courage to ask the nurse at the neurosurgeon's office about the feasibility. She had said she didn't see any issues. So, on this day, when he brought it up, I thought: *Why not give it a try? Maybe it'll actually be fun.*

And: *it's probably now or never.*

I'll spare you, reader, the details. Or maybe more accurately: *I'll spare myself the embarrassment of recounting it.*

Suffice it to say that cognitive confusion and ever-worsening short- and long-term memory are not conducive to emotional *or* physical intimacy. The whole encounter was *very* short-lived, and nowhere close to satisfying—in any way, shape, or form.

It was rather distressing, actually.

There was no way I was going to share this experience with readers on CaringBridge back when we were going through this. I hesitate to even share it here. But here's the thing: this is *real.* Caregiving is hard, and there are so many aspects that people are not willing to talk about. If someone feels a little less alone after hearing this account, or a little more encouraged to have honest conversations with their medical team, then including this experience will have been worth it.

Quick update on infection
September 10, 2015

Brief update: The doctor called today, and
they want to temporarily increase the oral
antibiotics to deal with the infection in the
short term, and reassess after next
week's MRI.

New MRI results; update on tumor and infection
September 17, 2015

This week Dennis had a new MRI, and we met
with both the neuro-oncologist and neurosurgeon to evaluate the tumor and infection. Here
is the net of it:

It appears there are areas of new tumor growth
in his brain. The infection is still present,
and is currently being kept at bay with
conservative treatment (high dose oral antibiotics). The only way to eliminate the infection would be invasive and risky treatments
(think two surgeries and a month in ICU--if
all goes well).

It appears that eliminating the infection
would have little to no benefit in terms of
either life expectancy or cognition. So, we

```
will continue with conservative treatment of
the infection.

Hospice is coming next week to help us plan
the next phase.
```

———

The status above seems to be pretty straightforward. Actually, it *is* pretty straightforward.

However, it did not seem all that straightforward at the time. Amidst talk of additional surgeries and other aggressive steps, it wasn't initially clear whether such actions should be undertaken.

Before a decision was made on the next step, Dr. Cobbs sat down with us and had a realistic talk about what to expect if we went the route of trying to clear the infection with additional surgeries.

"I've seen what a month in the ICU does to patients, and what it does to families," he said. "It's very difficult for everyone."

Once we talked through the options, it became clear that there wasn't really even a potential benefit to attempting this. It was neither going to help Dennis live longer, nor help his remaining days be better. In fact, it would make his remaining days worse. And potentially fewer, if surgical or ICU complications arose.

So, on this day, I ended my post with a simple sentence: "Hospice is coming next week to help us plan the next phase." I presented it as a standalone statement, without comment—as I'd done a few months prior when announcing Dennis's diagnosis of glioblastoma.

It didn't seem a momentous announcement. To me, it seemed the inevitable next—and final—step.

It seems, however, that the word "hospice" has clear implications. If anyone following along on CaringBridge hadn't been certain how dire Dennis's situation was, there now was no room for doubt.

60

ER again today--broken rib
September 21, 2015

Early this morning, Dennis fell in the shower.
We had to go to the ER via ambulance. Long
story short, he has a broken rib. No concussion. He is now resting at home.

O n this particular morning, Dennis had gotten out of bed
early—I think around 5:00 a.m.—and was trying to get
ready for work. This was an ongoing point of confusion. He
would often wake up and, no matter the time of day, think it was
time to shower, dress, and get ready to go.

When he got out of bed on this particular day, I woke up, too.
This was because the bed alarm went off when he got up. I was
half asleep, and heard him getting into the shower. I sat on the
edge of our bed to listen, and to be ready to help if needed.
Mostly, I wanted to go back to sleep.

The shower stool that had been provided by the physical therapist had been removed from the shower. He didn't like using it, and didn't remember that he was supposed to. The therapist and I had agreed it was probably safer to remove it than to have it taking up space in the small stall and creating a trip hazard.

All of a sudden, in my half-asleep state, I heard a loud "thud," followed by him crying out in pain. I flew into the bathroom and found him on the floor of the shower—he had slipped, apparently, and fallen. He couldn't get up.

I turned off the water and tucked some towels over him like blankets so he wouldn't get cold. And then I wasn't sure what to do. I really wasn't sure if I could lift him. And, even if I *might* have been able to, I wasn't really sure I *should*. I was worried about a potential back or neck injury, and whether I might make it worse by trying to move him.

So, I called 911. It was my first time ever calling them. I always imagined that if I had to call them someday it would be in the middle of some urgent, panicked situation —say, a robbery in mid-break in, or a heart attack in progress.

This was actually a rather calm call:

"911, what is your emergency?" the dispatcher said.

"My husband has fallen in the shower. He's in a lot of pain. He also has terminal brain cancer. I'm not sure what to do, so I thought I should call you. I'm not sure I can lift him, and I'm worried about making things worse if I try to. What do you recommend?"

She sent an ambulance. And, helpfully, she told me to unlock the front door before the paramedics arrived, and make sure the path from there to the bathroom was clear.

I realized that if I didn't wake up the kids and fill them in, they would awaken to medical personnel in the house, and they would likely panic. It was very early, and they were asleep. I knocked on their doors.

"Dad's OK, but he fell in the shower. His back hurts a lot, and he can't get up. I called 911 and they are coming to see if he needs to go to the hospital," I told each of them.

Of course he needed to go to the hospital. I called my parents to come stay with the kids and get them off to school while we headed to Swedish. From the ambulance, I emailed their teachers to fill them in on the morning's events.

It would turn out to be Dennis's last ER visit.

61

Broken rib, day 7
September 27, 2015

It's been almost a full week since Dennis
broke his rib. I won't beat around the bush;
it's been a difficult week. In fact, if I'd
written this post on day three or four, the
title probably would have been something like
"Broken ribs suck."

As I look back at all the skills and tasks
I've had to learn the past few months, I'd
have to say this is the hardest to manage by
far. Fortunately, he seems pretty comfortable
when he's not moving--so that is something,
anyway. But, any movement, such as getting out
of bed, has been excruciatingly painful for
him. This means that gaining his cooperation
so I can help him move about has been exceed-
ingly difficult--the result of which has been

a sore back and a sense of defeat for me. This
is the first logistical hurdle that I really
truly thought I might not be able to manage.

And yet, here we are on day seven, and it's
less-bad. We have some better pain management
tools. He can and does get out of bed (with
assistance). My back is less sore. We are
managing. We've had help and guidance from
family and friends, and now from hospice.

Speaking of hospice, that officially started
Thursday. I think it will be helpful. We are
still getting that ramped up, so I'm not
entirely clear who will be coming when, but at
least the ball is rolling on that, and we've
already had visits from their nurse, nurse's
aide, and social worker.

This broken rib has really been a bad deal.
It's remarkable how much he has declined--both
physically and cognitively--in just the past
week.

W hen you read that "this broken rib has really been a
bad deal," you should probably interpret that as *this
broken rib has been an unmitigated disaster.*

It was, truly, the first—and only—time I really, honestly
thought that I might not be able to do this.

I was forty-three years old, and I was taking care of my
husband with terminal brain cancer. The previous few months

had been full of surgeries, inpatient stays, emergency room visits, and more pills than I could count. Now it had become incredibly demanding—physically—to care for him.

I was already, practically speaking, a single parent—and had been since day one of this journey. I had a house, a dog, and a cat to take care of as well. I also had a full-time job as an IT project manager, working on large-scale, global software upgrades and deployments, and had recently started trying to work again after being off for quite a while.

Fortunately, I worked from home, and fortunately, my managers were extremely accommodating. I also had massive amounts of help in the form of meals being delivered, kids being carpooled, pets being walked, and so much more. But still, I was ultimately the one with responsibility for all four of our lives.

Physically I was exhausted, and my back was killing me. Mentally I was overwhelmed. Emotionally I was defeated.

I put some calls in to see if there was a hospice facility where Dennis could go. There wasn't. Why? Who knows. It doesn't really matter anyway.

I had to keep going.

Many things change when a patient moves from the medical system into hospice at home.

One of those is the arrival of new people on the scene.

Out were calls to the Ivy Center, visits to the ER, and prescription pickups at the pharmacy drive-through. Instead, we fell into a rhythm with regular visits from the hospice bath aide, the nurse, and sometimes, the social worker.

I remember when the social worker came for one of her first visits. Maybe the very first one. One of my close friends was there for moral support during the meeting, and the social worker was trying to assess how much help we had, as a family, for the path ahead.

I described the myriad types of assistance we'd been receiving from our community—some of whom, by the way, we'd already been close to. But others were fellow school parents, neighbors, friends-of-friends, or other acquaintances— kind people, all of them, who stepped up to help. You never know in situations like this who will end up in your corner.

The social worker turned to my friend.

"How long are you guys prepared to provide this support?"

"Until the end," she said quietly. And very definitely.

I am so, so lucky.

Once we got going with hospice, a whole new routine emerged. Dennis had daily visits from the bath aide. The nurse visited weekly—sometimes more often—and the social worker was in touch as needed. There was no more calling the doctor's office for me. No more trips to the ER.

If ever I had a question, or Dennis had a problem, I would call the 24/7 hospice phone number. They could give advice, and quite often would send an on-call nurse to examine and address things like fevers, pain, or signs of infection. They would call and consult with the doctor's office when needed.

Hospice also supplied a new hospital bed, which was pretty much identical to the one previously arranged by the insurance company. But, of course, swapping one for the other was a bureaucratic necessity. They also brought helpful things like a rolling tray table for the bed, and eventually some fancy mattress topper that was supposed to head off bed sores. They provided all the medication and other supplies we needed.

They also gave me the hospice "Little Blue Book."

It was more of a booklet than a book. It was written by a hospice nurse in 1985, and the official title is, *Gone From My Sight: The Dying Experience*.

Yes, it's as awful as it sounds.

And yet, it's oh-so-helpful. It describes, in great detail, what happens when someone is dying. What to expect in the preceding weeks, days, hours, minutes.

Please don't read it until you have to. And then, please be sure you do.

62

Very brief update
October 5, 2015

Very brief update:

- Dennis is now bedridden; he is still at
home.

- He seems to be feeling OK. Rib only hurts
when moving.

- Boy Scouts came to our house for an awards
ceremony for Peter yesterday, so that Dennis
could be part of it.

- We have started working with Safe Crossings,
an organization which provides grief support
for kids. Wonderful so far. And the kids do
really get what is going on.

I will try to elaborate more in coming days;
too tired now.

Many thanks to everyone who has been
supporting us at home, whether with meals,
kids, keeping Dennis company, or hands-on
help.

————

I know I said that the kids really did get what was going on. I
think they *mostly* did.

Dennis, however, did not. His day-to-day life didn't change
much with the transition to hospice. He was still camped out in
a hospital bed in our lower-level family room. Visitors
continued to come into our home to see him. The TV remained
a near-constant companion—because it was something to do,
and because it gave everyone something to chat about.

Speaking of visitors, I took to reminding Dennis who people
were when they came, because I wasn't really sure who he might
or might not recognize. I tried not to make a big deal about these
cues. I'd usually bring a guest downstairs to see him and say,
"Hey Dennis, so-and-so is here! You remember them, of course,
from such-and-such!" He'd smile and say: "Hello! Yes!"

Did he recognize any of them? All of them? I'll never know.
His long-term memory held up better than his short-term
memory throughout his illness, but by the end his long-term
memory was mostly gone, too. If I could prevent the embarrassment of all parties by making a quick comment, it seemed the
thing to do.

. . . .

There was one aspect of caregiving that was introduced around this time that I never wrote about in my posts: diapers. The closest I got to mentioning the topic was in this entry when I thanked people who were providing "hands-on help."

Maybe the need for diapers seemed too personal. Or too undignified to discuss.

But, like the aforementioned attempt at physical intimacy, this aspect of terminal illness was *real*. It was hard. And it wasn't Dennis's fault.

I'm quite sure he wouldn't have chosen to give up his independence and rely on me to change his diapers several times a day. Me and a helper, that is—because it turned out to be a two-person job. Every time this task needed to be done, I had to call a family member or friend to roll him on his side, while I did the rest of it. I had a short list of go-to people who were willing to help with this. Sometimes I'd call at 10:00 p.m., and one of them would drop everything and come over.

In any case, once Dennis was bedridden, diapers—and a Foley catheter—became a necessity.

One more thing they don't tell you about caregiving ahead of time.

I started this chapter by saying I thought the kids *mostly* got what was going on. But, in hindsight, I wish I'd known more about how to talk with them about it. That it was important to be checking in with them, even if they *seemed* OK. That it was alright for them to feel sad or mad or worried or whatever, and that I didn't have to try to "fix" that. That I just needed to listen, to hold space for them and those feelings.

I think it would have set us up better for the next phase.

The phase when we'd have to figure out how to start living again, after Dennis died.

63

The power of community
October 14, 2015

Recently I watched a clip of Joe Biden talking
with Stephen Colbert about the death of his
son, Beau, from brain cancer. He said he was
so lucky, in the midst of such tragedy, to
have such wonderful family and friends to get
him through it. He recognized that so many
people suffer all kinds of tragedies in their
lives without nearly the support network
he has.

I have to say, I feel the same way. Things
could be so much worse for us: we could be
facing the same circumstances ... alone. Or
with minimal support. And that would make a
terrible situation so, so much worse.

Instead, by way of example, let me tell you

about today. (Admittedly, today was a bit
unusual. But still.)

- First, the hospice bath aide was here for
daily clean-up.

- Next, Dennis's mom was here. She made him
breakfast and visited.

- Then a friend of Dennis's visited. They
played cards and watched football.

- After that, a friend of mine was here. They
watched more football, and she walked the dog.

- Next, a couple of long-time family friends
were here. They visited, and we discussed the
home improvement projects on the agenda when
they return in a couple weeks.

- While they were here, a cleaning lady
arranged by St. Louise friends came and did
wonderful work.

- After work, four people from Dennis's office
came to visit with him. They brought food, and
a photo book of people and projects from the
office.

- While they were here, another friend dropped
by with homemade breakfast burritos for the
freezer.

- Oh, and in between all those things, another
friend both picked up the kids for school, and
dropped them off after.

That's a total of thirteen people today. Wow.
We are so lucky.

We are settling into a bit of a "new normal."
(I recall writing a post months ago with that
title ... I guess that was a bit premature.)
Dennis remains in bed. He remains cheery. He
remains confused. He seems to be stable.

He has visitors, watches TV, and reads the
paper. He enjoys the card game "war." He loves
the family photos, taken by a photographer
friend, that I got framed and up on the walls
last Friday.

Hospice nurses, aides, social workers, and
chaplains are in and out. Insurance is working
to arrange some additional hours of home care,
which will be wonderful for all involved. The
kids go to school and activities, and I work.
The kids are learning Photoshop so they can
make creative photo books for Dennis.

I made only brief mention in my last post of
the Court of Honor held here for Peter weekend
before last. Peter was ready to "rank up" to
Second Class. Since Dennis will be unable to
attend the upcoming Court of Honor (nor any
other Courts of Honor, for that matter), about

twenty scouts and adults from Peter's troop
came to our home, in uniform, to hold the
ceremony so that Dennis could attend. First
they did a Board of Review (a panel of adults
interviewing Peter, a requirement for rank
advancement), followed by the awards ceremony.
The scouts were so kind to come. I know Dennis
enjoyed it, and Peter will always remember
that his Dad was able to attend this Court of
Honor.

Part of the "new normal" has been that I have
been trying to get to bed earlier. I've basically been getting everyone tucked into bed,
doing all the nighttime meds and what not, and
then falling into bed myself, with Megan
sharing my bed (which makes getting her to bed
sooo much easier). In fact, I was already in
bed at 10:00, but then I started thinking
about this post and decided to get back up. I
guess I had better get back to bed, now that
it's after 11.

Here is the Biden interview with Colbert:
bit.ly/biden-colbert-interview

————

We had such a tremendous outpouring of support
during the eight months Dennis was sick. It was
incredible.

We had family. We had friends. Old friends, new friends,
friends-of-friends. Colleagues. Neighbors. School families.

People near and far. It seemed that everyone wanted to help, to support, to follow along. It made a huge difference.

It did not make a difference in the outcome. No matter how many casseroles we got, no matter how many times the dog got walked, no matter how much was chipped in to hire someone to clean the house—nothing would fix the brain cancer. That's the nature of glioblastoma. As I've shared, it's insidious.

But—it helped *us*. It helped me bear the burden. It helped lighten our load. It took everyday tasks off my plate, so I could concentrate on medical and emotional tasks. It helped us to feel we were not alone. And it made it possible for three, of the four, of us to survive Dennis's terminal illness.

Which was, after all, the best outcome we could realistically hope for.

64

Six months
November 1, 2015

It's November 1. Exactly six months since I
first noticed symptoms (May 1).

I haven't posted an update in over two weeks.
Truth is, there isn't much to say. Just wanted
to let you all know we are still here, and to
thank you for your support and caring for the
past six months.

A half of a year. Yikes. I'm tired.

———

Yep. So, so tired. And feeling like I was living in the movie
Groundhog Day.

Because, by now, just about every day was literally *the same*.
Wake up. Make sure the kids were ready when carpool

arrived. Fix some eggs for Dennis. Turn on the TV for him. Write up the medication schedule for the day, based on what time he woke up and got his first doses of his multitude of meds. Try to squeeze in some work, usually made possible because someone had come by to hang out with Dennis for a few hours. More meds. More food. More TV.

Some days, visitors would drop by. Some days, the hospice nurse or aide would come to check on him. We'd discuss what additional meds or supplies needed to be ordered. These are the sorts of days that passed for "eventful," at this point.

And then, evening. Evening meant, first of all, heating up something that a meal train volunteer had dropped off. Then more hanging out in front of the TV. And finally, bedtime meds —including administering a shot with blood thinners—and usually a diaper change, too. Then I'd turn on the borrowed baby monitor—necessary so I could hear Dennis if he awoke in the night—turn off the lights, and head up to bed myself. Oh, and somewhere in there I'd get the kids into bed, too.

Then I'd wake up the next day, and do it all over again.

It seems odd, now, to realize that what started out as every-day-or-two posts six months earlier had become sporadic updates. We still had just as many people supporting us. Just as many wanting to stay in the loop.

But the truth is, by this point, I had very little to say. Nothing much to report. I didn't want to bother people by posting the same non-news day after day. And I wasn't in the sort of mood for writing reflective posts, either.

The end was approaching—only I didn't know when it would arrive. The only thing for me to do was keep going, one day at a time.

65

Brief status update
December 3, 2015

The main focus lately has been pain and
comfort management. It is hard to figure out
where Dennis's pain is and what is causing it,
because he's unable to articulate what he's
feeling, where it hurts, etc. Maybe it's his
head. Maybe it's the abdomen. Maybe something
else. Maybe all of those.

At any rate, we're now on a regimen of
morphine every twelve hours to try to keep it
in check, plus additional morphine as needed
for so-called "breakthrough pain."

Also, he seems generally weaker, is still
eating but is eating less, and sometimes needs
help eating. His energy level and voice volume
are low.

I know it's been a while since I've posted.
Thanks for staying with us.

————

By now, Dennis had been on hospice for about ten weeks. One day—who knows when, with all the days blending together by then—the hospice chaplain called and asked to come by. I didn't know why I should meet with him, since our pastor at St. Louise had been in the loop from the beginning. But I figured, *what could it hurt?*

We met in my living room for our first—and, I should say, last—meeting. Dennis was in the other room, probably with one of the many friends who came to keep him company and give me a break from round-the-clock caregiving.

I mentioned to the chaplain my intention to speak at Dennis's funeral. I didn't know when it would be, but he had been diagnosed with the thirteen-month-average-lifespan brain cancer six or seven months earlier, and had recently become a hospice patient. I had been kicking around possible remarks for a while at that point—primarily when I went walking.

Walking had always tended to be when I'd do my clearest thinking. I used to compose papers in my head in college, while walking, returning home only when I'd worked everything out and just needed to type it up.

I was ninety-nine percent sure I wanted to speak at the funeral. But, the hospice chaplain tried to talk me out of it.

"You don't want to make things harder on yourself than they already are," he said—presumably thinking he was being helpful.

I began second-guessing myself.

Here was a guy who knew a lot more about death than I did. Maybe he knew something I didn't? Maybe there was something

I didn't know about funerals that would make my plan impossible. Or unwise. Maybe I needed to listen to the "expert?"

I don't know why he gave the advice he did. I suppose he typically worked with widows much older than I; maybe they didn't often make remarks at their husbands' funerals. Maybe he just thought, "Here's this poor woman with two young kids, she doesn't need one more thing on her plate."

But—he didn't know me. He didn't know that I'd been writing since the beginning of Dennis's illness, sharing our journey with family and friends near and far. That seventy-eight posts and twenty-nine thousand site visits later, I needed to speak to the people who'd been supporting us for so long. I needed to reflect on my husband's life, and I needed to thank our community for their role in this, the hardest time in my family's life.

And so, I thanked the chaplain for visiting, and we wound up the conversation. I desperately wanted to ignore his advice, but he had planted a seed of doubt that continued to gnaw at me in the weeks and months to come:

Could he possibly be right?

66

Rough week; rough night
December 13, 2015

Last night was rough. Dennis was really having
a hard time. Lots of pain, lots of pleading
for help. It turned out that the catheter was
clogged. A hospice nurse came and replaced it
(which was painful, but fortunately the
painful part was accomplished quickly). I
think he finally left here around 1:00 or
1:30 a.m.

The rest of the week was also rough. Very up-
and-down, actually. There were times he was
low energy, not very alert, not able to feed
himself, etc. Then there were times that he
was remarkably improved. Keep in mind that
"improved" is relative. Like, there were a
number of times when he expressed an entire
sentence with startling clarity. Such as:

Me: "How's it going?"
Dennis: "OK. Better than you might think."

I just about fell over. It might not sound
like much, but his vocabulary has mostly been
limited to "yeah," "oww," and sometimes "I
don't know" for a while now. So to hear him
say something "normal" like a full sentence in
the right context was remarkable.

The kids are handling all this so bravely.
They went to a Christmas gift making workshop
after school this week. They were both excited
to make gifts for Dad. As soon as they got
home, Megan asked if she could give Dennis her
present right then, "in case Daddy dies before
Christmas." She did give it to him, and was so
excited and proud to do so. We have re-wrapped
it so she can give it to him again on Christmas, because he won't remember that he already
opened it.

Both kids have been so encouraging and
supportive. Megan was trying to help me with
his pills last night. He has no problem tech-
nically swallowing, but very often holds the
pills in his mouth and does not drink the
water, no matter how much cajoling and prod-
ding we do. (Today I put the pills in apple-
sauce, which helped.) Megan was so sweet,
trying to help him: "It's OK Daddy, let me
hold the cup, just put the straw in your
mouth and take a drink. Open your mouth, let

me see if you swallowed them." Peter likes to
get him cookies, and wind up the music box
snow globe for him to enjoy. Both are unfail-
ingly cheerful, positive, and helpful when
around him.

Dennis is exhausted today, and sleeping a lot.
Here's hoping for a better week for us all.

I t breaks my heart to remember now that Megan wanted to
give Dennis the gift she made at school right away—*in case
Daddy dies before Christmas.*

And, that we both thought it logical and reasonable—to
wrap it back up so she could give it to him again on Christmas
morning. Because he wouldn't remember that he'd already
opened it.

Thus was our reality.

Also, part of our reality was that Dennis needed a lot of care.
He was at home, so the kids were witness to this. And, for the
entire eight months, they were so cheerful, positive, and helpful
with him. I think I was relieved that, for the most part, they
weren't acting out. That took a whole set of potential problems
off my plate.

But here's the thing—there's no way they really could have
been fine with it. Peter might have brought Dennis cookies with
a smile, but my guess is he was freaking out on the inside.
Megan might have cheerfully persuaded him to take his pills,
but she must have been an internal mess.

I'm glad they helped their dad when he needed them. I'm
glad they had a positive attitude while doing so. But I wish I'd
made time during those days to check in more with them. To

start a conversation. Once again, to let them know that it was OK to be sad, and OK to be worried.

It could have been as simple as, "Hey, I really appreciate your help with Dad. I know he does too. I'm guessing this must be awfully hard (or scary, or confusing) for you, though."

Even if they didn't want to talk about it, just opening that door would have sent the message clearly enough. And eventually, maybe, they would have shared how they were feeling.

In any case, by mostly deferring the difficult conversations, it made my job after Dennis died that much harder.

I try not to beat myself up about it, because know I was doing the best I could. I had a lot on my plate. But mostly, I didn't know any better. I didn't know what I was "supposed" to say. Or do. Or not say, or not do.

Those unknowns paralyzed me.

I needed a guide, and it was painfully obvious to me that I didn't have one.

67

Save the date: Seattle Brain Cancer Walk
December 16, 2015

I'd love to have you all join Team Dennis for
the Seattle Brain Cancer Walk on May 1, 2016.
Details to follow later.

———

At this point, shortly before Christmas, May was a really long way off. I knew in my gut that this, our first time attending the brain cancer walk, would be in Dennis's memory —rather than in his honor. Somehow, I knew he'd be gone by then.

I was still just *hoping* that he'd make it to Christmas. I remembered all too well that Megan had asked, way back when the doctors first said it was brain cancer, whether he would still be with us for the holidays.

All I could say at the time was: *I don't know. I sure hope so.*

Oh, how I wanted this to be true.

. . .

In the meantime, we busied ourselves watching Christmas movies on the Hallmark Channel. Their oft-repeating schedule turned out to be handy, as I frequently missed the beginnings or endings of shows when I was in and out of the family room throughout the day. Of course, it's not hard to figure out what's going to happen in any of the stories—but I didn't have to guess, as it would be easy enough to catch whatever I'd missed the next time any particular movie aired.

The rapidly approaching Christmas holiday also presented a gift-giving conundrum: what exactly does one buy for one's dying husband, who won't live long enough to get much use out of the gifts he receives? It's not like you can pull a *Seinfeld* and say "no soup for you." As impractical as buying gifts was, the alternative was unthinkable.

I settled on a selection of T-shirts that I thought Dennis would find meaningful—Huskies, AC/DC, Star Wars, and the like. Unfortunately, his hospice aide promptly took scissors and cut open the backs of the shirts—something they apparently do to facilitate more easily dressing patients who are bedridden. This, of course, ruined the shirts for any long-term use—such as passing them down as keepsakes for the kids.

At least Dennis got to wear them for a time.

68

Christmas cheer and caroling
December 17, 2015

Local friends: You're all invited to our home
for family caroling this weekend.

Two times to choose from: Saturday at 7 p.m.
or Sunday at 7 p.m. We'll do it twice, so
hopefully friends who want to join are
able...twice the fun for us!

Please dress warmly, as we will be primarily
outside due to space constraints. We will
have a patio heater, camp fire, hot chocolate,
and adult beverages. We'll open the patio door
so Dennis can join in the festivities.

Megan's Girl Scout troop came and caroled this
week with a similar format, and Dennis really

enjoyed it...and was even singing along.
(WOW!)

RSVP preferred, if possible.

So much fun caroling. Please join us tomorrow!
December 19, 2015

So much fun caroling tonight. Thanks to all
who were able to join us. Once we finished
with the Christmas songs, we continued the
singalong with some John Denver and other old
favorites. Peter was in charge of the fire,
and Megan the food and drink table. I played
guitar. Dennis was tired, but seemed to
enjoy it.

If you are able, we'd love for any and all of
you join us tomorrow (Sunday) at 7 p.m.!

Perhaps a new tradition
December 21, 2015

I'm sitting here with blistered fingers
(haven't been playing guitar much lately...)
and thinking about how much fun I had caroling
and seeing so many friends here at our house
the past few nights. I was so glad to host a
little party, and to sing with everyone.
Someone mentioned that this caroling party
sounded like a lovely tradition. I think we
need to make this year one of a new tradition!

Sunday was much the same format as Saturday,
with the crowd a bit larger. It was also cold-
er...but miraculously, the rain held off. (It
poured all day today.)

Tonight some of Dennis's colleagues came over
to visit. They brought dinner and dessert, and

we did some more caroling. Dennis was singing
along with a few of the songs ("Deck the
Halls" was one, if I remember correctly).

Dennis has been struggling lately with an
infection, and nurses were out twice this
weekend dealing with catheter issues. Today we
finally got labs back, and started another
antibiotic. Hopefully that helps make him more
comfortable.

———

I have such fond memories of these caroling parties. They
were such a bright spot in an otherwise dreadful time.

I can't remember now if these get-togethers were my idea or
someone else's. They may have been my sister's idea. In fact, I
think they were—and, as I recall, I initially thought she was
crazy.

But you know what? It was awesome.

I got immense joy out of planning, and hosting, them. Joy
that was probably disproportionate to the inherent nature of the
events, and certainly not commensurate with the overall state of
things.

I loved having a chance to play guitar and sing with people. I
loved the idea of hosting a little party for those who had been
with us all the way. And that's how I thought of it: *I'm hosting a
little party*. It was so *normal sounding*.

And, I thought it important to try to bring Dennis some
Christmas cheer, on this, what would certainly be his last
Christmas.

He even sang along at a few points. It was wonderful.

71

After the bright spots that were the caroling parties came the Christmas holiday itself.

If I'd only had myself to think about, I probably would have skipped Christmas.

But, I had Dennis to consider. This was to be, without a doubt, his last Christmas, and it didn't seem right to deprive him of it—even if he probably wouldn't have noticed.

Plus, the kids. It didn't seem fair to cancel Christmas on them, just because their dad was dying. So, we made a valiant effort to celebrate the holiday.

I say "we" because I certainly didn't do it alone.

Earlier in December, someone had stayed with Dennis while the kids and I went to cut down a Christmas tree at the local tree farm. It was probably someone from the caregiving agency that I'd recently managed to arrange for eight precious hours a week, paid for by Dennis's insurance.

I was conscious that this outing to procure a tree—with just the three of us—was foreshadowing my future as a single-mom-to-be. I was determined not to hand the saw to Peter—then eleven—and assume that he would take on what some might consider the "man's job" of cutting it down.

Sure, he was male—but I was the *adult*. So, the three of us took turns cutting. I don't remember who did the lion's share—probably me—but the point I wanted to convey to my kids was that I was capable of cutting down a Christmas tree, and that they were *both* capable of contributing to the family effort.

With the freshly cut tree at home, we turned to decorating. My mom helped with inside adornments, and my dad and Peter worked on the outside lights. In addition to the usual decorations, a small tree was set up for Dennis in the family room, and an illuminated snowman figure placed outside the patio door where he could see it.

With that, our home was festive in presentation, if not in reality.

The holidays notwithstanding, cancer and hospice were still very much front-and-center in day-to-day life. I had to order a pill crusher from Amazon on Christmas Eve—for same-day delivery—because Dennis stopped swallowing pills. Just because he wouldn't swallow them didn't mean he could stop taking them. Christmas Eve dinner happened because my parents and my sister's family handled everything. Presents turned up under the tree, because my neighbor came over late on Christmas Eve—after everyone was in bed—and helped me finish wrapping the gifts, all of which I'd ordered online.

The same neighbor also snuck a few extra presents under the tree for me. Several friends had gone together to procure them, since they knew Dennis wouldn't be doing any shopping that year.

The day after Christmas, the kids and I had tickets to see the brand-new *Star Wars Episode VII: The Force Awakens*. The release of the first episode of the new trilogy was a *big* deal that December. There hadn't been a new *Star Wars* movie in a decade; presumably the saga had come to an end with the release of the final prequel in 2005.

Dennis was a huge *Star Wars* fan. The original movies, Episodes IV, V, and VI, came out when we were kids. When the first prequel, Episode I, was released, we were newly married and living in New York. He was *so* excited to see a brand-new *Star Wars* movie in the theater, sixteen years after *The Return of the Jedi*.

Thus, when *The Force Awakens* came out, it seemed inconceivable that only three-quarters of our family would go see it—and that Dennis wouldn't even know what he was missing. I thought about skipping it altogether. But, the buzz around it was *huge*. Peter and Megan wanted to go, and Dennis, being completely bedridden at this point, didn't have the option of coming with us.

I could have told him there was a new *Star Wars* movie and that I was taking the kids to see it, but I didn't see the point. He probably would have been sad—or I would have been—and then he would have forgotten all about the conversation five minutes later.

So, I purchased three tickets—carefully timed to work with the four-hour window when I could arrange for a caregiver—and off the kids and I went.

We didn't talk about how weird it was to go without dad. We just went.

You may have noticed that this chapter didn't start with a journal entry. I don't know why I didn't post at the time about any of the goings-on of Christmas and the surrounding days.

Maybe it all felt too sad. Or too pedestrian. Maybe I was overwhelmed. Or maybe, by the time each day ended, all I could do was fall into bed—and not stay up one minute longer to compose anything for the people following along on CaringBridge.

Status
January 8, 2016

Dennis is in a coma. Fever. Labored breathing.
I expect we'll lose him today, or maybe this
weekend. He is at home, and does not seem to
be in pain.

73

Rost in peace Dennis
January 8, 2016

We lost Dennis this afternoon after his eight-
month battle with brain cancer. We all love
and miss him very much. He passed peacefully
at home.

The funeral will likely be late next week.
Details will be posted here.

Thanks to everyone who has offered their
prayers, best wishes, and assistance.

———

As I said before, it strikes me now as a bit odd that I didn't
write at all between the previous post on December 21—
about our caroling parties—and these two posts on January 8,
saying first that Dennis was in a coma, and then that he had died

that day. In between we had a span of eighteen days, including both Christmas and New Year's. As Megan had so desperately hoped, way back when we first learned that his tumor was cancer, Dennis was still with us for both of these holidays.

By this time, our regular hospice nurse was coming with increasing frequency. We also had a number of visits from on-call hospice nurses to address urgent issues. Each day was filled with a schedule of pills, shots, meals, and whatever else cropped up.

I do know that time slows down tremendously during something like this. My world was confined to basically the four walls of my house, plus a rotating crew of visitors, including family, friends, and the hospice team. My main touch point with the outside world was the online journal.

It was a lifeline.

When I was living through this period, I had not realized how close together all these major dates were. Basically, Christmas was one Friday, New Year's the following Friday, and Dennis died the Friday after that. So, all this in a span of just two weeks.

I only realized how much time had slowed down when the *following* holiday season rolled around. The first without him.

I had a headache—an actual, literal headache—straight through from that next Thanksgiving until the day after Dennis's death anniversary.

74

Funeral arrangements
January 9, 2016

The funeral mass for Dennis will be Friday, January 15, at 11:00 a.m. at St. Louise Parish.

Reception immediately following in the parish hall. Party at our home in the evening. All are welcome and encouraged to attend.

———

Here's something they don't tell you about planning your husband's funeral: if you pick songs you like, it will ruin those once-favorite songs for you. It will be impossible to hear them again without thinking back to the funeral. With flashbacks, in my case.

Fortunately picking songs was, for the most part, the easiest part of planning Dennis's funeral. I was reminded that, several years back, a family friend had reached out for help in identifying songs for a Catholic funeral for her own husband. She was not Catholic herself, so was looking for ideas on what would be appropriate. Dennis was happy to help, and had emailed me a list of suggestions so I could forward them to her.

Here's the weird part: he ended with an editorial comment that he hated to bring up something so sad, but that should I ever find myself in the position of needing to plan his funeral, these would be songs he would want included.

I searched my inbox and found Dennis's old email without much trouble. I stared at my screen in disbelief—it was as if he was speaking from the grave.

I still had to pick a song or two, as he hadn't identified enough to cover all the song needs. The school choir would be singing, and I knew they did a beautiful job with "Go Make a Difference." *Go make a difference. We can make a difference. Go make a difference in the world.* I knew he would have loved this as the recessional. I loved it, too.

The problem is, now I can't stand hearing it anymore. Especially from the lovely school choir. It hits way too close to home.

In addition to music, there were readings, readers, cantors, and Eucharistic ministers to choose. An obituary to write. Funeral-appropriate attire to procure. Remarks to prepare. All made more difficult because, as soon as Dennis died, I came down with a *major* cold. It was as though my body had been hanging on through all the ups and downs of the prior eight months—and then crashed as soon as my role as a caregiver came to an end.

Fortunately, the staff at St. Louise was experienced, and also recommended a funeral home that had done many funerals in the parish. This meant their coordination was smooth—and most importantly—didn't require me to get in the middle of it. I was comfortable that the church and funeral home staffs knew each other well and were used to working together. This was a big weight off my shoulders. After so many months of being responsible for nearly *everything*, I could just make the decisions that I had to make, and leave others to oversee many of the details.

75

Additional details for Friday
January 11, 2016

On Friday, we will hold three events celebrating Dennis's life:

(11 a.m.)
Funeral Mass at St. Louise Parish church.

(Immediately following Mass)
Reception in parish hall, downstairs from the Church. Many thanks to the St. Louise funeral committee and school parents for organizing and running the reception.

(5 p.m. +)
Party at our home. This will be a combination celebration of life and a thank you to the wider community for your phenomenal support over the past eight months.

Party will be "Soup Night," as we hosted so many times when we lived in Portland. Dress warmly as it will be an indoor/outdoor party.

Many thanks to my sister's friends for organizing and bringing food for the party. To answer many who have asked: if you'd like to bring something, please bring a beverage to share.

Children and adults welcome at all events. Looking forward to seeing many friendly faces on Friday. If you think you may be coming from out of town, please message me.

————

When Dennis and I lived in Portland, Oregon, we started a monthly Soup Night at our house. Peter was probably around a year or year-and-a-half at the time, and we really wanted to connect with other young families in the neighborhood.

The format was simple: Each month, we made a different homemade soup, plus canned chicken noodle for the kids. We asked guests to bring salad, bread, beverage, or dessert. It was a standing invitation to a group of families, most within easy walking distance of our home, and a few a bit farther afield. We were never quite sure how many would show up, but it was generally in the range of fifteen to thirty people.

Soup Night was such a wonderful way to build connections with friends and neighbors. And it was such a defining element of our time in Portland. When we moved back to Seattle, we really missed the tradition. We never got it started again here.

And so, after Dennis died, I just knew I needed to host a Soup Night for our community. For the many people who supported us throughout the eight months he was sick, and those who traveled here to support us for the funeral. Plus, it would be a great excuse to buy the gigantic stock pot I'd seen at a nearby restaurant supply store.

I had in mind that I would make the soup for this party. Dennis had always made the soup at our Portland parties; now it would fall to me. Of course, it was ridiculous to think that I would make *all* the soup for a large party on the evening of my husband's funeral. Or really, it was probably ridiculous that I would make *any* of it—but I was determined to do so. I realized, probably wisely, that I would have to "cheat" a bit, and bought some bullion broth powder and canned beans. I think I chopped the carrots and celery; I know I put a visiting relative to work chopping onion. I remember getting the soup started on the stovetop, before a friend implored me—wisely—to let her take over so I could tend to other matters.

A bunch of people had come over in the days after Dennis died to get the house ready for the out-of-town guests who were coming for the funeral. The family room, which had held his hospital bed, had to be restored to its normal configuration, and the accompanying bathroom purged of hospital supplies. I remember the hospice nurse instructing me that I'd have to dispose of the leftover medications, but that I couldn't just throw them away or flush them, as some were serious narcotics. She suggested things like putting the pills in a bag of used coffee grounds to destroy them. Fortunately, a couple of my friends were there and stepped in to say they'd take care of it. *One more thing off my plate.*

My sister's friends kindly stepped in to do much of the party prep and execution. They re-arranged living room furniture to make room for a crowd, set up outdoor tents (it was January, after all), and organized people to bring crockpots with other soups—along with salads, bread, and who knows what else. They set up and strategically placed large garbage cans. They procured a keg. And they helped throughout the evening, keeping things rolling smoothly.

I have no idea how many people showed up. Hundreds, I guess. All I know is that, around five o'clock, when people were due to begin arriving, I stepped out onto the deck to find the keg and fill my red plastic cup. One of the first guests was there when I turned around, so I had someone to talk to. I was standing in the same spot for at least the next hour, as guest after guest arrived and came outside. I'm not sure if they were looking for me or the keg, but either way, pretty soon the deck was packed.

At some point I headed back inside and was shocked to see how many people were jammed into my 1,750 square foot house. The main floor was like a college party—you couldn't move. Literally. It was crazy. I hope I saw everyone over the course of the evening. I have no idea.

Eventually the crowd thinned, and out came the guitars. It must have been at least midnight by this time. Chairs were rearranged to make a large circle in the living room, and I took up a spot on the couch between my two aunts. Others in my family—who had come from near and far—were gathered in the circle, too. A few friends were still there at that point. It will always mean so much to me that they stayed.

What happened next, I will always remember. The family sing-along. Right in *my* living room. What I remembered from my childhood. What I'd been singing along to on the CD recording of my aunts and my dad.

I'd been playing guitar—and singing—for less than three years at that point. I'd borrowed an extra guitar from a friend so that my aunt would have one to play, since she had flown in and wasn't able to bring her own. And we played Kenny Rogers's "The Gambler" together. We had to play it in my key, not hers, because I was not that experienced of a guitar player and couldn't change what I knew.

It was amazing.

Equally amazing was harmonizing to "Leaving on a Jet Plane" with my other aunt. And singing so many other old family favorites: "Mamas Don't Let Your Babies Grow Up to Be Cowboys," "Charlie on the MTA," "Life's Been Good," and so many others. Some obscure, but everyone in my family knows all the words, more or less.

I wonder if some of my friends thought we were nuts. But I loved it.

Dennis would have loved it, too.

76

Megan's welcome remarks today
January 15, 2016

Thank you everyone for coming.

My dad was very thoughtful and kind.

He would be happy that all of you are here.

I will always remember how my dad taught me
how to make scrambled eggs, fried eggs,
poached eggs, and omelets. The reason I'm
telling you this is that not a lot of kids
know how to cook those things. My dad was
great that he taught me how to make them.

Thank you so much for coming and celebrating
with us.

I wasn't sure Megan would be able to give the welcome at the funeral. It required getting up in front of hundreds of kids and adults, including *all* of her classmates, and being the first speaker of the day. It's a lot of pressure even for an adult to speak at a funeral, and she was just nine at the time—and this was her dad.

She was, however, determined to do it.

As the week wore on, she resisted my efforts to prompt her to consider her remarks. Thank goodness for the children's grief counselor from Safe Crossings, an organization affiliated with our local hospice. She had started coming to see the kids at the house partway through Dennis's illness, probably around the time he started on hospice.

In the days before the funeral, she was able to sit down with Megan in a way that I wasn't, and get her to think about what she wanted to say. The counselor asked Megan what she thought, and wrote it down as Megan dictated it. In relatively short order, they were done.

On the day of the funeral, I asked Megan's godparents if they would accompany her to the podium. I thought she could use the moral support of having them stand with her. Also, they had a copy of her remarks, and the backup plan was for one of them to read her welcome if she backed out at the last minute.

Megan delivered her remarks herself. Short and sweet, it turned out to be a warm way to welcome everyone and set a friendly tone.

There were many people—including lots of children—in attendance. Because our kids attended the Catholic school associated with the parish where the funeral was held, all the kids' classmates—all third and sixth graders in the school—attended. That was around a hundred kids, plus their parents, and some families with kids in other grades as well. Add in other friends, family, Dennis's colleagues, etc., and it was a large, mixed-age group. The school choir did the music. Long-time family friends —a girl Megan's age and her dad—were the cantors. Girl Scouts and Boy Scouts wore their uniforms. You might say it was a family-friendly funeral—so having Megan give the welcome turned out to be just perfect.

I'm so proud of Megan for getting up there and doing it.

77

Jenny's remarks today
January 15, 2016

Wow. What a great group.
It's great to see so many friendly faces here
today.

You know, when I was in college, and I had to
write a paper,
maybe five or ten pages,
I would walk.

I would start at my little apartment on
Capitol Hill, in Washington D.C.,
and walk all the way to the Lincoln Memorial
and back.
A walk of maybe a few hours.
And as I walked, I composed my paper in my
head.
By the time I got home, my paper was done,

and I just had to sit down and type it out.

Now--before I continue--let me say to the
students here:
I don't want your Language Arts teachers to be
mad at me!
I'm sure you're learning how to write a proper
outline and such.
So please don't follow my example.

But, it worked for me.

And so this week,
as I was thinking about what I wanted to say
to you all today,
I laced up my shoes,
and I walked.
I walked and walked around my neighborhood.

And I was reminded of a quote
that I came across when I was in college in
Oregon.

It was this:

"If only I could give you one gift,
I would give you the ability
to see yourself
as others see you.
Only then would you realize
what a truly special person
you are."

And I realized--I've been given a gift.

I know the man I married.
I know the man I love.
I know the man who was so proud to be Peter's
and Megan's dad.

And now, I've been given the gift
of seeing Dennis
as others saw him.

As I've read through the many messages
that have come in over the past week,
and actually over the last eight months,
a portrait of Dennis appeared
that I'd like to share with all of you today.

It seems that people saw Dennis as a
family man.

One person said:
"I have such fond memories of Dennis from St.
Louise and loved seeing his posts about you
and the kids. He was so proud of you all."

Another said, when he was in the hospital a
few months back:
"I can see when I visit that he is not
confused about his love for his wife and
family."

And someone else said:
"I will always remember Dennis as a kind and

gentle man who demonstrated to me what being a father means. He was smart and thoughtful and always fun to talk to. You, Peter, and Megan were so fortunate to have this man in your lives."

I couldn't agree more.

It also seems that people knew Dennis as a kind and gentle soul.

One person said:
"I went to high school with Dennis and can only smile when I think of him because he always had a smile for everyone else. Truly a gentle soul, filled with kindness and generosity for all those around him."

A childhood friend said:
"When I first moved into the cul-de-sac, Dennis was kind and welcoming. Though he was a little bit older than me, he made me feel like I belonged. We rode our bikes and played baseball in that cul-de-sac for many summers and weekends."

And someone else said:
"Dennis was always so nice to me. Always friendly, conversational, engaged, and clearly believed in community and kindness, as evidenced by your wonderful soup nights."

Again, I couldn't agree more.

Finally, it seems that people thought they
were better off for having known Dennis.

One person said:
"I'm thankful our paths crossed 11 years ago."

Another said:
"It's an honor to have known Dennis--a very
fine, gentle, and intelligent man with a great
smile and eyes deeply kind. I know when I hear
AC/DC, I'll think of him."

And someone else said:
"We are privileged to have known Dennis."

Again, I couldn't agree more.

I know that I am a better person for having
known him.

I also know that I'm a better person for
having known all of you.

You have all been phenomenal in your support
over the past eight months.
I wish I could thank you all by name.

But, I know that with the stress I'm
under now,
I'd likely omit someone.
And I could not bear the thought
that someone might leave here today

thinking that their kindness was unnoticed or
unappreciated.

So, instead, I will say,
if the shoe fits, wear it.

I remember the first time I heard that
expression,
when I was a kid,
I was kind of puzzled by it.
But then my dad explained,
that if someone says something like
"everyone needs to make sure they are keeping
their rooms clean,"
then one ought to think about that,
and if it applies to them,
then take it to heart.
And if it doesn't, then don't worry about it.

And so I want to say to you all today,
if the shoe fits, wear it.

If, for example, you brought us a meal, or a
bag of groceries,
or made a Costco run--
or especially if you brought chocolate ice
cream or York peppermint patties--
or if you stopped by in the evening with a
bottle of wine and conversation,
then the shoe fits you.

Please accept my thanks and gratitude.

And if you carpooled our kids to school,
took them to sports or Scouts,
provided school lunches,
had them for a play date or sleepover,
or if you or your kids showed them kindness
and friendship
during our ordeal,
then the shoe fits you, too.

If you helped Dennis,
if you visited him in the hospital or nursing
home,
if you took him to radiation,
if you came over to watch the Mariners,
Seahawks, Huskies, or Food Network with him,
if you hung out with him so I could work, or
take the kids somewhere,
or if you helped me with caregiving tasks when
he was bedridden,
then the shoe fits you, too.

If you worked with Dennis,
if you sent cards from the office, visited,
contributed to shared leave for him,
or held down the fort while he was out,
then the shoe fits you, too.

If you built something, fixed, installed, or
painted something,
cleaned or organized something,
weeded, mulched or planted,
picked up the mail, took out the trash cans,

contributed to the housekeeping fund, or
helped with the dog or cat,
then the shoe fits you, too.

If you reached out with a kind card, email,
text,
social media message, or phone call,
or if you kept us in your thoughts and
prayers,
whether or not you reached out,
then the shoe fits you, too.

If you prayed, laughed, cried, or sang
with us,
perhaps at a Rosary gathering,
or at one of our caroling parties,
then the shoe fits you, too.

And if you helped us prepare for today,
whether it was by helping with parts of the
Mass,
by helping organize or bring food for the
reception or the party tonight,
or by helping us run around and find funeral
clothes,
then the shoe fits you, too.

Please accept my thanks and gratitude.

I know I can't possibly repay your kindness.
And so, I will close with the words to a song
that was popular when some of us were young.

If you ever find yourselves in crisis,

Lean on me
when you're not strong
I'll be your friend
and I'll help you carry on.

As so many of you
have done for me.

Thank you all so very much.

And speaking of songs,
Dennis loved The Beatles,
and one of the songs that I practiced for
myself this summer
was their song "Let it Be."

And so, I'd like to invite you all
to join me in a sing along,
downstairs during the reception,
of "Let it Be."

We can lift our voices high,
and hopefully Dennis will hear us.

Thank you so much for coming today.

E very time I re-read the remarks I made at Dennis's funeral, I reach the same conclusion:

I wouldn't change a word.

I have to admit, though, that a little part of me had been wondering—right up until the moment I began speaking—whether the hospice chaplain had been right when he tried to talk me out of it.

When I got to the podium, I looked at the large crowd assembled in the church, sighed audibly, and said, "Well, I guess it's my turn."

This was not the opening I'd written down, but it sure reflected how I felt.

Peter oh-so-helpfully mentioned later that might not be the *best* way to start a talk in the future.

I don't have audio or video of my remarks, and I think that is probably just as well. I want to remember it through the lens of that day, relying on my memories to characterize it for myself. I'm fairly certain that if I had a recording, I'd watch it now and feel my delivery was a little flat. I also wish I'd delivered it without notes.

Mostly, I am satisfied that I trusted myself on this one.

Through my writing, I'd been sharing our experiences and my in-the-trenches reflections over the past eight months. Fifteen thousand written words later, I needed to pull it all together, and I needed to put voice to my experience.

I'm so glad I didn't let that hospice chaplain dissuade me.

78

Obituary
January 17, 2016

Dennis Wilfred Lisk, Jr., of Redmond, died on
January 8, 2016, at his home after being diagnosed with brain cancer in May, 2015. He was
44 years old.

Dennis was born on July 19, 1971 in Everett,
Washington, son of Denny and Elba Lisk. He
grew up in Bellevue and attended St. Louise
Parish School and Sammamish High School. He
received his undergraduate degree in History
from the University of Washington in 1993, and
his Master's degree in Urban Planning from New
York University. He married Jennifer Doman on
July 18, 1998.

Dennis loved his job as a senior planner for
the City of Redmond. He was proud to work on

many interesting and innovative projects for
the betterment of the city. He loved spending
time with his family. Together they enjoyed
camping, hiking, and golfing. He loved to cook
and eat good food, and took pride in cooking
for his family. Dennis will be remembered as a
kind, gentle soul.

Survivors include his wife Jenny Lisk, children Peter (11) and Megan (9), mother and
stepfather Elba and Dan Raven, sister Tracy
(Lisk) Brown, brother Christopher Lisk, and
many extended family members.

There will be a funeral mass at St. Louise on
Friday, January 15, 2016 at 11:00 am.
Following the service there will be reception
for family and friends in the parish hall.

The family suggests remembrances to the Ben
and Catherine Ivy Center for Advanced Brain
Tumor Treatment or Holt International Children's Services.

Friends are invited to share memories and sign
the family's online guest book at
flintofts.com.

———

There is really only one thing to say here: writing an
obituary for your forty-four-year-old husband just sucks.

79

Seattle Brain Cancer Walk: Join us?
April 19, 2016

Please join us if you're so inclined: one mile walk on Sunday, May 1, to raise money and awareness for brain cancer research. All welcome. Kids too.

The team is called "D's Dawgs," named for the Huskies, of course. Wear your best purple and gold if you can join us. :)

Thanks to Dennis's sister Tracy for setting up the team.

———

After Dennis died, I never wanted to hear the words "brain cancer" again. Brain cancer had already taken up too much of my life, and taken too much from my life. It took up eight terrible months—eight months of medical drama, pain, sadness, and stress—and in the end, it took my husband of seventeen years. And it took my kids' dad.

I had spotted the "Seattle Brain Cancer Walk" poster on the wall of Dr. Cobbs's office way back at one of those early visits to the Ivy Center. The 2015 walk had just occurred, and my interest, at that time, was more hypothetical—as in, *oh, wouldn't that be a nice cause to support?*

By the time the 2016 walk rolled around, it was *personal*. And personally, I had close to zero interest in participating. After the year we'd just been through, my energy level was low, and my desire to hole up at home was high.

Dennis's sister offered to create a team. I decided that if she did all the organizing, I could probably manage to get myself and the kids there.

I'm so glad we did.

We've been four times now, and it turns out that the Seattle Brain Cancer Walk is a joyful event. There's live music, free food, and lots of people. The walk is more of a stroll than an athletic event. Mostly, it's a celebration of—and fundraiser for—the groundbreaking research that Dr. Cobbs is doing on potential viral causes of glioblastoma, potential vaccines for it, and more.

The disease has received a fair amount of attention in the mainstream press in the past few years, which is good for highlighting the critical need for research. Senator John McCain was the most recent high-profile glioblastoma patient, having died in 2018. Before that it was, as previously mentioned, Beau Biden. Some years prior, Senator Ted Kennedy also died of glioblastoma.

For years now—decades, maybe—survival rates for glioblastoma patients have not fundamentally improved. For most patients, such a diagnosis is still a death sentence. In spite of this, I actually do know someone now—a new friend—who survived glioblastoma. I have no idea how. She's one of the lucky few, I guess.

There are some new treatments now with some promise. And, Dr. Cobbs has made a groundbreaking discovery of what looks like a virus that causes glioblastoma. The next step is to develop some sort of vaccine against it. We're not there yet.

Before Dennis had his first surgery, he granted permission for his tumor cells to be used in Dr. Cobbs's research. Here's hoping that, one day, he will have played a tiny role in finding a cure.

PART III

PICKING UP THE PIECES OF OUR LIVES

80

TURNING INWARD

When Dennis died, I felt an overwhelming need to turn my focus inward. Not go anywhere. Not see anyone. Not have a house full of people, as we'd had for the previous eight months.

Don't get me wrong, I really appreciate all those people who were in and out of our house and lives while Dennis was sick. It's just that, after he died, I'd had *enough*. I needed time and space to reclaim my home and my little family and my thoughts.

I also had the drive to nest. One of my first projects was to clean out my closet and paint my room. Like so many others around that time, I had been reading Marie Kondo's book, *The Life Changing Magic of Tidying Up*.

I need some life changing magic. If tidying up can bring me that, then bring it on.

I did pretty well with the closet. I had gotten rid of some of Dennis's things while he was on hospice. That might sound weird. To me, by doing it then, I was *getting rid of things Dennis didn't need*. At the same time, I was getting rid of many *things I didn't need*. I knew if I waited, the nature of the task would change to *getting rid of my dead husband's things*—which sounded a lot worse.

I really had just gotten rid of stuff I was sure he'd never want, even under normal circumstances—like clothes that were old or worn out, or that he didn't wear any more. The same types of things I was purging for myself.

After he died, I took the plaid button-downs that he wore to work every day and put them in a plastic tote labeled "Dennis's old shirts." These were saved to make quilts for the kids someday. I put some special items, like his Seahawks jersey and NYU sweatshirt, into another bin to save. I saved some good gear, like Gore-Tex rain pants, for Peter to wear when he got a little bigger. I put other clothing that we didn't really need for regular use into the emergency backpacks—stuff like extra hats, raincoats, and wool sweaters. I figure that if we ever get a really bad earthquake—"the big one"—here in Seattle, then we'll haul out the emergency backpacks and be grateful to have, and wear, Dennis's old things.

I took all my own clothes, shoes, and accumulated junk out of the closet—per Marie Kondo's instructions—and piled it all on my bed. It was a big mountain. I also took out all the old falling-apart shelves, leaving the closet totally empty and bare.

I went to Ikea and got closet organizer units with hanging space, drawers, and shoe racks. I painted the walls—ceiling too —and built the pieces. I had to call friends to help me move a few heavy items into place—something I'd always had Dennis help with. It would be a while before Peter would be strong enough to help with tasks like this—and a real adjustment to realize I'd now need to call a friend whenever I needed an extra set of hands.

By the time I went through the mountain on my bed— throwing out anything that was old, tired, I never liked anyway, or didn't "spark joy"—I hardly had anything left. After more than a decade of working from home, I had virtually no work attire. Other things didn't fit or were out of style. I finally made tough decisions, being honest with myself about what I would really wear, and got rid of the rest. In the coming year, I would rebuild my wardrobe a few pieces at a time.

I painted the walls of my room, too, and got new super-comfy jersey sheets—and finally felt like I had a place to nest.

It wasn't just painting my room I had to take care of in the weeks before I had to go back to work. I had paperwork, matters with the estate, and so many phone calls.

Please cancel my husband's cell phone. He's dead.

Can you change the cable bill to my name?

What do I need to do with these joint bank accounts to get them into my name alone?

It seemed like the list was endless. Actually, it *was* endless. I still get junk mail in Dennis's name all the time. I also, inexplicably, still get the property tax bill in both of our names, even though the county reissued the house title in my name only. And they didn't make that change recently, either. It's been years.

I also get letters all the time, addressed to Dennis, asking if he wants to increase his existing life insurance before his rates go up.

Um—yes, please?

And yes, I've called them. It hasn't stopped the solicitations from coming.

81

EARLY STEPS FORWARD

After the initial flurry of activity, it was back to work. And back to life.

Or, not "back." There was no *back* to go to. Only forward.

We'd been through eight months of hell. Now the rest of my life was staring me in the face. And the rest of the kids' lives, too.

Since there was no "going back" to the way things were, my next-best wish was that the three of us not become collateral damage to Dennis's cancer.

The best medical professionals attacked his cancer—but as I've said, glioblastoma is insidious. They couldn't fix it.

This did not *necessarily* mean that we had to be destroyed, too.

I was determined that this not be the case.

The first months were, for me, filled with flashbacks. Every time I tried to concentrate on working from my home office— not ten feet from my husband's urn—my mind would begin to wander. Generally, it wandered into flashbacks.

It was like I had a VCR looping in my head. (Can you tell I'm a child of the eighties?)

Scenes of the emergency room. Of the surgery waiting area.

Of inpatient stays. Of driving across the bridge to Swedish. Of the hospital bed in our family room for so long.

And—of the funeral. This was the most recent, and there were so many "scenes" from the funeral playing on a looping tape in my head. Me standing at the front, giving my remarks. Recalling who sat where. Remembering their faces. Processing in, recessing out. The school choir singing.

So many flashbacks.

What I didn't have were those "waves" of grief that people talk about. You know, the ones where all of a sudden, you're fine, and then grief washes over you like a wave.

I didn't understand what was wrong with me. Isn't that what grief is "supposed" to feel like?

The kids' grief counselor from Safe Crossings continued to visit our home after Dennis died. She and I got to know each other in the course of her working with the kids, as I asked questions about how to help them, and such.

One day, when I mentioned the flashbacks I'd been having, she said to me, "I think you might be an instrumental griever."

"What's that?"

"It's someone who tends to process grief more cognitively than emotionally."

Yes. That's me. One hundred percent.

I went straight to Amazon and searched for "instrumental griever," and ordered the one book that came up. It's a fascinating book called *Grieving Beyond Gender: Understanding the Ways Men and Women Mourn.*

The main point is that grievers can be classified into "intuitive grievers" and "instrumental grievers." Intuitive grievers are the ones who experience the waves of grief, and they process grief more emotionally. Instrumental grievers tend to process it more mentally, including playing scenes over and over in their heads.

It's a continuum, so people can exhibit both tendencies, in varying degrees. Here's the interesting part though: women tend to be intuitive grievers, and men tend to be instrumental grievers. But this is not always the case. There are both men and women in each type.

The tricky part is that society generally expects men and women to fall into certain types. And grief groups tend to be structured for the dominant grieving style of the gender.

Finally, I understood why I kept turning down my friend's invitations to the monthly grief group at Swedish. She kept reaching out—which was very kind—and I kept saying, *no, I don't think so, I don't feel like it this month.*

Eventually I asked:

"So what do they do at this group? Sit around and talk and cry?"

"Well, yes," she said.

"Yeah. I don't think that's going to be for me."

Don't get me wrong, I love talking with people. And I cherish time with my widow friends. But somehow this group didn't seem quite right for me.

I'm not sure why. And, I'm sure it's quite helpful—even exactly the right approach—for many people. As an instrumental griever, it just didn't seem like a good fit for me.

Fortunately, I have found a group of widowed friends who live nearby. We get together at someone's house, or we go out. The discussion is wide-ranging. Grief comes up, and so does laughter. Work. Parenting. And whatever else is on anyone's mind.

I'm so lucky to have these ladies in my life.

. . .

Gradually, I came to realize that what I needed was a guide. Someone or something who could tell me how to do this new job called "widowed parent."

Because I felt totally lost.

I found that there are *many* resources for adults dealing with their own grief. I'm not saying it's easy, by the way—I'm just saying that there are books. There are therapists. (I found an amazing one.) There are online and in-person groups. There's even something called "Camp Widow."

With all these supports and more, I could see that I would eventually be able to find a path forward.

When it came to parenting, though, one of the most frustrating aspects of my new reality was not knowing where to turn for answers.

Answers to questions like:

Is this current issue my kid is facing a grief issue or a normal kid issue?

Do I need to try to (somehow) force a kid to do an activity they don't want to do, like play on the basketball team or go on a family outing? What if they don't want to do it because they're sad about Dad? Does that matter?

Is it OK for my kid to sleep in my bed? For how long?

Does my kid need a grief group? Where do I find one?

What if I think my kid needs more help? How do I begin to untangle the options for mental health support? How do I find someone who is knowledgeable, and a good fit for my child?

And, most importantly:

Who can even help me answer these questions?

So, I did what seemed logical to me: I went looking for the book that would tell me what to do. How to raise grieving kids while grieving myself. How to support them and—hopefully—not completely ruin their lives. How to do this thing called "widowed parenting."

I could not find such a book. Don't get me wrong, there *are* lots of great resources out there—but they are fragmented. There are skilled therapists, grief camps for kids and teens, and, in many cities, grief centers with excellent programming. These should definitely be called upon, as they are a tremendous resource for grieving children and their families.

But, in the immediate aftermath of Dennis's death, I didn't know about most of those options. I felt just as lost as I had when he was sick and I didn't know where to turn for advice on parenting through terminal illness. Now that he had died, I wanted to find one resource that would help me understand the "lay of the land" of widowed parenting. Start me in the right direction. Tell me what I needed to know right away, and help me learn what might come up on the path ahead.

After all, if your kid goes to a therapist weekly, a peer grief group monthly, and a grief camp for a few days in the summer— which would be a lot of grief work, by the way—there are still somewhere around three hundred days in the year where it's all on you, the widowed parent, to figure out what to do.

I needed to find a guide.

82

FINDING MY WAY

In the weeks and months following Dennis's death, I was paralyzed by the lack of a road map. Something that would show me how to do this thing called widowed parenting. It was a job I didn't sign up for, but one I now had nonetheless.

And I then realized—I couldn't be the only widowed parent feeling like this.

With that epiphany, my desire shifted. No longer was my agenda just about seeking answers to help my family survive. Perhaps, I thought, I could seek out and interview people who could begin putting into place the various pieces of this puzzle. Perhaps I could even deliver these lessons to *other* widowed parents. And maybe—just maybe—I could do that in the form of a *podcast*.

Soon, I became passionate about the prospect of creating something to help others who were struggling, too. I could use my background in technology—even though none of it was directly related to podcasting—to fill a gap that I saw in the world.

At the same time, I was racked with doubt. Deep down, I questioned:

Why me?

Who am I to host a podcast on widowed parenting?

After all, I'm not a therapist, or a parenting expert, or even a widowed parent whose kids are now grown. I'm very much in the trenches—right now—with this.

And then it hit me:

I'm the Kevin O'Connor of widowed parenting.

Perhaps you're asking yourself: *who is Kevin O'Connor?* He's the third—and current—host of *This Old House*, a show on PBS that preceded my now-favorites on HGTV. When Dennis and I bought our first house—a 1921 fixer-upper in Yonkers, New York —we were totally obsessed with *This Old House*.

Right around the time we were religiously watching, they switched to their third host. The first two hosts had been experts —but with Kevin, the model flipped. He was intentionally *not* an expert. He was an enthusiastic DIY homeowner-type, and he stood in for the audience, asking questions of the show's resident experts in each episode.

That's when I realized: it's actually better that I'm *not* an expert on widowed parenting. No one wants a show where I preach at them each week on what they should be doing. A much more effective format would involve me inviting experts on the show, standing in the place of my listeners, and asking questions on their behalf.

And that's when it hit me: what started out as a quest to find answers for my own family had become a calling. I *had* to look for answers—and I *had* to share them with others like me.

By now, I was getting serious about starting a podcast. But—I didn't know what it would look like. Could I turn it into a job? Did I need to go back to school and get some sort of credential to make an impact? Could I even afford to?

I desperately wanted to make a career change, to leave Corporate America, to do something that felt, to me, more meaningful. I'd tired of spending my days working on internal financial systems, and longed to help widowed parents like myself.

I wasn't sure I had the guts to.

You see, ten years before I'd also been seriously entertaining a career change. I had the idea that I'd go back to school and become a nurse. I studied the program requirements, and enrolled in Psych 101 at Portland Community College—near our home at the time—because it was a prerequisite for nursing school. Each Wednesday evening, thirty-five-year-old me—possessor of both bachelor's and master's degrees—went off to a freshman-level psychology class with the eighteen- to twenty-two-year-olds.

It was fascinating. I loved every minute of it.

But, when push came to shove, I didn't see how I could make a major career change work. It didn't seem realistic to shift from being the primary breadwinner with a tech salary to bringing in an entry-level nurse's salary. After all, we had a house, a dog, and a mortgage—and two kids to raise. Conventional wisdom said it would be irresponsible to step away from the apparent security and advantages of my well-paying job.

Fast forward a decade, and I faced a similar conundrum: did I have the courage to ditch my corporate job—and the life it funded—for a chance at existential happiness?

Soon my hand-wringing was moot—my employer forced the issue.

Like many tech companies, they had jumped on the business trend known as "co-location." This is the belief that teams perform better when they sit shoulder-to-shoulder. The decade they'd spent singing the praises of a virtual, global workforce notwithstanding, a couple of years after Dennis died, they issued an ultimatum: Keep my job and relocate to the New York suburbs, or part ways.

I actually briefly considered relocating. I'd worked in that building before, having started my career there twenty years earlier. Since I was familiar with the area, more for fun than anything, I started looking at real estate online. I found a cool house that was ten minutes from the office, and began envisioning my kids starting sixth and ninth grades at the local middle and high schools, respectively.

My online real estate meanderings came to a screeching halt when I looked at the photos in the listing—an attractive colonial-style home—and saw a split-rail fence which, while charming, would not contain our dog. So much for that idea.

But really, it came down to this: I couldn't fathom relocating. Most family members, and many friends, were in the Seattle area—with some just a stone's throw from me. We'd finally felt established. With the kids starting middle and high school, it didn't seem a good time to tear them away from our community.

And, not insignificantly, it seemed really weird to relocate to the exact same part of the world—and exact same office building—where Dennis and I had started our big adventure shortly after getting married. I'd be going back there minus my husband, plus two kids.

On top of all that, it didn't seem sensible to relocate for a job I fantasized about leaving, and from which I might eventually be laid off, anyway.

If moving back to New York was eliminated from consideration fairly quickly, another possibility loomed large: looking for a corporate IT job in Seattle.

This, after all, might have been the responsible thing to do. I had twenty years' experience, a strong track record, and an

MBA. There were many tech employers in Seattle. Presumably I could find a position with one of them.

I couldn't bring myself to do it.

It's not that the work didn't suit me, exactly—it's that I felt pulled toward turning my loss into something meaningful.

A local corporate job also sounded somewhat impractical, given my new status as a solo parent. I'd been working remotely, and on East Coast hours, for nearly fifteen years—a schedule which was incredibly helpful and flexible in terms of family needs. And that was a time when there were two parents in this family.

As a now-single mom, would it really work to go to an office all day, every day? And add commute time on both ends? When would we eat dinner? Could I cover the inevitable days the kids would be home sick? Was everyone doing well enough that I could be away from home that much?

When push came to shove, I had to get really honest with myself:

Would I work to support my comfortable lifestyle, or would I work to make the world a better place for widowed parents—even if it meant potentially compromising that lifestyle?

Once I got clarity on the question, it became easier to see the answer.

You see, Dennis died—*but I didn't*. Living as he did to age forty-four, he got something like half of a life. If I live the rest of my life kind of half-heartedly, it would almost be doubly tragic.

And I felt like that is what I had been doing—and would continue to do, if I didn't make a significant change.

So, now, I had to choose what was next for me. And ... I *got* to choose.

Somewhere in my post-loss obsessive reading binge, I stumbled across the idea that one should imagine life in five years, and ask themselves this question: *if my life is the same five years from now as it is today, would I be OK with that?* If the answer is no —or especially if the answer is *hell no*—then *now* is the time to do something about it.

I told the world I was taking a one-year sabbatical to see what I could do in the area of widowed parenting. I figured I could always go find another tech job in a year if it didn't work out.

I was pretty sure I wouldn't be exercising that escape hatch.

83

FINDING MY VOICE

I got to work setting all the necessary balls in motion to start a podcast. I made a list of potential guests. Got cover art for listing my program in podcast directories. Studied the formats of shows I liked, learned how to edit audio files, and hired a voice-over guy to make the intro and outro.

Finally, the day arrived. My very first podcast interview.

I'd been hoping to interview a friend of mine first. As it turns out, I have several neighbors who are widowed parents—including my across-the-street neighbor, who had been widowed for over a decade at that point. She was kind enough to agree to an interview back when the podcast was still just an idea, and I really wanted to dip my toe into the waters by speaking with her first.

I figured that if everything was a disaster with this first interview—the sound quality was terrible, I failed to lead a compelling discussion, or I forgot to hit "record," for example—I could probably lean on her to do it all over again.

Instead, I dove off the deep end.

By happenstance of how the schedule came together, my very first interview was with a complete stranger. Someone I had been following on Instagram and reached out to when I was trying to line up guests for the first few episodes. And I was nervous.

You see, I'd never interviewed anyone before. Literally *never*.

So, I did what any resourceful person with access to a computer would do. I thought to myself, *who is the best interviewer I can think of?*

And then, I Googled: "How to interview like Terry Gross."

Armed with my new insights as to how the host of National Public Radio's "Fresh Air" approaches her work, and a way-too-long list of questions for my guest, I started the interview.

Soon we were engrossed in conversation. I looked at the clock after a while, and realized that I had absolutely no idea whether we'd been talking for twenty minutes, or an hour and twenty.

I finally hit the "stop" button on the recording.

And at that very moment, I was overcome with the sense of liberation that comes from *finally* seeing the value of your life—and of your work.

In that moment, I knew there would be no turning back.

It's funny how an everyday object can take on an entirely new meaning when circumstances change.

The laptop—that indispensable tool of my time in Corporate America—had once tethered me to a career in which I felt stuck and unfulfilled.

When Dennis got sick, and my world shrank to the four walls of our house and of his hospital room, the once-utilitarian laptop elevated its standing. It opened for me a portal to the outside world.

Day by day, post by post, I began looking beyond myself and

communicating with my corner of the world through my online journal.

Nearly three years after Dennis died, I added a mic to the laptop—and after I got one interview under my belt, I instinctively knew:

I had found my voice.

With my voice now located, only one task remained: to really and truly accept that my future was mine to define.

And so, one day, as I shifted in my chair for what must have been the fiftieth time in our typically-hours-long discussions, I posed the ultimate question to my therapist.

It actually wasn't so much a question as a statement.

A rhetorical question.

An *a-ha moment.*

I flipped through the notebook that I usually toted along to these meetings so I wouldn't forget any of the topics I wanted to tee up. I reviewed my chicken-scratch notes on the page, took a deep breath, and asked out loud, to myself as much as to her:

If I don't own my own life, who the hell else will?

The look on her face said it all.

This was *the* question.

The one staring me in the face for so long. The one I had to ask in order to find myself.

Find my voice.

Find my way forward in the face of tragedy.

And—the beautiful thing about it?

The moment I asked myself this question, I realized I already had my answer.

EPILOGUE

Four years after Dennis died—while working on this book—the perfect opportunity to consider how far I'd come as a widowed parent presented itself. *Star Wars: The Rise of Skywalker* would be in theaters at Christmas time.

This, the ninth and final installment of the big-screen adventure that had begun forty-two years earlier, became my symbolic test: had I learned enough in the years since Dennis's illness—a time when I'd felt completely lost as a parent—to help my young family survive the hand we were dealt?

You'll recall that when Dennis was home on hospice, I took the kids to see *The Force Awakens*, the first part of the final trilogy. Two years later, we got tickets for the sequel when it came out. Neither time did I have the fortitude to address the elephant in the room: how weird it was to see the new *Star Wars* movies without Dad. I was afraid to bring it up. Afraid of the discomfort of such a discussion, and of the potential emotional fallout.

Now I was getting yet another shot at it. A mulligan. A chance to apply the lessons I'd since learned about grief, and parenting—and do better than before.

This time, I deliberately provoked a conversation with Peter:

"I was able to get tickets for *Star Wars* this weekend. Saturday at 7:30."

I can never remember which of the newer episodes is which, so I tend to call them all *Star Wars*.

"Sounds good."

"You remember, of course, who was a big fan of *Star Wars*?"

"Dad."

"Yeah. Sure seems weird to be going without him."

I added, for good measure, how strange it had felt to go without Dennis when he was sick, too. Peter agreed. We talked about it, and got the awkwardness of what we were both thinking—but not saying—out of the way. It was an important moment—and one that cemented what I'd learned about the importance of honest discussions.

Finally, I'd proven to myself that I could have the hard conversations. That doing so was preferable to ducking them. That holding my breath and *hoping* to avoid an uncomfortable topic wasn't the best course of action. I wish I'd known this much, much sooner.

Better late than never.

Today, five years after Dennis's death, my life looks totally different than it did before. Instead of toiling away for a large technology company, which I did for twenty years, I now run my own show. Quite literally. I find guests for *The Widowed Parent Podcast*. I read their books, and prepare questions. I edit the audio, and do all the social media outreach.

And I love it.

One might think that reading about, and discussing, grief and death all day long would be depressing. To me, it's not. I love talking to people about their ideas and their journeys, and —most especially—sharing what I'm learning with other widowed parents.

It is the sharing that is, to me, the most important. It's why I started the podcast, and it's why I wrote this book. I felt totally lost, both as a *future widow* and as a *newly widowed parent*—and I didn't want others to struggle as I have.

I'm able to share tangible, accessible information with my listeners, because I've learned so much from my guests on the show.

For example:

I've learned that it's critical to be honest with kids about difficult topics. Grief is hard, and death is uncomfortable. No one wants to talk about it. But, I've learned that our kids need us to try. They need to know that they can come to us with questions, and they need to know that we will answer them honestly. It's important that kids can trust their surviving parent, and honesty is integral to that.

I've also learned that it's OK not to have all the answers. As a parent, it's tempting to think that I should. After all, we're conditioned to carry this responsibility from the earliest days of parenthood.

Why do I have to sit in my car seat? Why do I have to go to school? Those are easy enough to answer.

But what about the questions that are impossible to answer? *Why did Dad have to die?*

There are no good answers to that one. You can—and should—explain any facts available to you, such as helping kids learn how cancer affects a person's body, or what happens when someone is cremated, if they ask about those things.

But when a question doesn't really have an answer, I've learned that the best approach is to try to connect with your child around their emotions, recognizing their feelings, and maybe even sharing some of yours: *I don't know why Dad had to die. I really wish I did. I sure miss him, and I can tell that you do, too.*

I've also learned that it's OK to be a "good enough" parent.

It's easy to feel that we somehow need to be the *perfect* parent after our spouse dies. After all, our kids have already gotten the short end of the stick by losing one parent at a young age. It's understandable that we'd feel we need to be perfect to compensate for that hardship.

As it turns out, nothing could be further from the truth. What our kids need is for us to be present, available, and warm. To model how we handle our own emotions, and to let them feel theirs. And if they experience some distress because not everything is perfect, that's OK—they need to learn how to handle that, too.

I've also learned that grief support for kids and teens is important. Many people want to believe that kids are resilient—and to some degree, they are. But it's not realistic to think that *all* kids will just "bounce back" from a major loss without any type of support. Some will, certainly. Others will need *much* support going forward, perhaps for years to come. The vast majority are probably somewhere in between, and would benefit greatly from connecting with other kids with similar losses, and learning to integrate their grief into their lives in healthy ways.

There are grief support organizations for kids and families in many communities. The National Alliance for Grieving Children, which has a listing of programs in every state in the United States, is a terrific place to start. Their website is listed in the resources section at the end of this book, along with a few other sources of online, downloadable information that parents of grieving children will find helpful.

Last, but definitely not least, I've learned that I'm not alone. I ask all my guests on the show to wrap up our discussion by answering one question: "If you could say one thing to newly widowed parents, what would it be?" It's remarkable how many answers contain some version of this essential message: *you are not alone.*

But, I know, widowed parents often *feel* lost and alone, and uncertain as to how to support their kids. It doesn't have to be this way. I started the Widowed Parent Podcast to help widowed parents everywhere increase their family's well-being—because every child deserves a chance to thrive, even if their parent has died.

I'm incredibly grateful that my guests on the show have shared their insights with my listeners, allowing all of us to learn from their experiences and expertise. And so, now, I continue to press on every day, trying to build a new life for myself and my kids. One that I didn't ask for, one that I didn't expect—but one that can be great nonetheless.

I hope that you will, too.

ACKNOWLEDGMENTS

To the community that surrounded us when Dennis was sick—the St. Louise School parents and staff; Dennis's colleagues at the City of Redmond; my colleagues at IBM; and family and friends, old and new, near and far: thank you for helping us survive the worst eight months of my life, and for showing me what it means to be an ally to those in crisis.

To the team at Swedish Medical Center, including especially Dr. Charles Cobbs and his team, and Mallory Higgins: thank you for taking such good care of Dennis, and for the critical research you're doing into viral causes of glioblastoma. Keep up the good work.

To Diane Dela Cruz, my first-grade teacher: thank you for giving me a strong start in school.

To Dennis Garrity, my high school social studies teacher: thank you for being the first to tell me you saw something special in my writing.

To Susan Leeson, my college political science professor: thank you for teaching me to write concisely.

To Dorie Clark and the Recognized Expert community, and Fei Wu and the Creative Entrepreneurs community: one of my goals since leaving my corporate job has been to meet people like you —*interesting people doing interesting things*. Thank you for your encouragement and your tireless example. I learn so much from you every day.

To my guests on the Widowed Parent Podcast, past and future: thank you for sharing your journeys with my listeners, and for teaching us all so much.

To the members of my launch team, including those who read this book early and shared advance praise: thank you for your generosity and your enthusiasm in helping spread the word about *Future Widow*.

To Julie Lythcott-Haims: I have heard you describe memoir as an act of service. Every time I questioned why I was writing this book, I stared at the sticky note on my wall where I captured this sentiment. Thank you for the work you're doing, which inspired me to push through when the going got tough.

To Jana DeCristofaro: I'm so glad you reached out about doing a podcast swap. Thank you for believing in me, and in this book— and for writing the foreword in the midst of pandemic, wildfire, and global chaos. Keep up the great work with your Grief Out Loud podcast.

To Jocelyn Carbonara: thank you for obsessing over every word in the manuscript, right along with me. This book is immeasurably better because of your comments, your questions, and your editorial eye.

To Tammy Gooler Loeb: thank you for being my writing accountability buddy, and for talking sense into me every time I questioned why I was writing this book.

To Nicole Antich, Leanne Arsenian, Wendy Clough, Lisa Greene, Stephanie Ottaway, Natalie Remedios, and Katie Rempe: thank you for being the best widow friends ever.

To Cathy Callans: thank you for helping me process the world around me, including grief.

To Renee Craddock, Ingrid Flaat, Jenny Roth, and Shawna Shaules: thank you for walking through life with me, then and now.

To my parents and all my family, near and far: thank you for your presence, your love, and your example. I got lucky with this family.

To Peter and Megan: thank you for allowing me the privilege of being your mom. You're the reason I do what I do.

To Dennis: thank you for the honor of being your wife. Your life was far too short; I promise to make the most of mine.

AUTHOR'S NOTE

To write this book, I drew from my CaringBridge journal, written from May 2015 to April 2016, and from my own memory of events. Some entries have been shortened or omitted in service of readability. Portions of the book that contain dialogue represent my best recollection of those conversations rather than exact quotes.

RESOURCES FOR FAMILIES

The Dougy Center
  dougy.org

Eluna Network & Camp Erin
  elunanetwork.org

Hamilton's Academy of Grief and Loss
  hamiltonsfuneralhome.com

National Alliance for Grieving Children
  childrengrieve.org

Widowed Parent Project
  widowedparent.org

MORE FOR READERS

Tips for widowed parents:
   jennylisk.com/topten

Tips for caregivers:
   jennylisk.com/caregivers

Tips for supporting friends:
   jennylisk.com/allies

Book club discussion questions:
   jennylisk.com/bookclubs

THE WIDOWED PARENT PODCAST

The Widowed Parent Podcast is your guide to "only-parenting" after the loss of a spouse. After losing her husband to brain cancer when her kids were nine and eleven, host Jenny Lisk decided to set out each week in search of the best information, advice, and experts, and bring them straight to fellow widowed parents.

The Widowed Parent Podcast features interviews with:

- Experts in the grief and loss fields with resources for widowed parents
- Stories from those whose parents died when they were young
- Reflections from experienced widowed parents

Listen in Apple Podcasts, Google Podcasts, Spotify, or your favorite podcast player.

widowedparentpodcast.com

ABOUT THE AUTHOR

Jenny Lisk is an author, speaker, and host of *The Widowed Parent Podcast*, which has been featured in the *Washington Post* and *ParentMap*. On her "Hundred Dreams" list is riding a camel. And milking a cow. And raising $44,000 for brain cancer research, in honor of her husband's forty-four years. She is passionate about helping widowed parents increase their family's well-being. Jenny lives in Redmond, Washington, with her two teenagers. This is her first book.

Please visit her website at jennylisk.com and connect with her on social media @liskjenny.

CPSIA information can be obtained
at www.ICGtesting.com
Printed in the USA
LVHW101921150522
718837LV00002B/240